CELEBRATING
(ADOPTION)

+ THE INTENTIONAL FAMILY +

KIMBERLEY RAUNIKAR TAYLOR

BEACON HILL PRESS
OF KANSAS CITY

Cover Design: Chad A Cherry
Interior Design: Sharon Page

All Scripture quotations are taken from the *New American Standard Bible®*
(NASB®) © copyright The Lockman Foundation 1960, 1962, 1963,
1968, 1971, 1972, 1973, 1975, 1977, 1995. Used by permission.

Library of Congress Cataloging-in-Publication Data

Taylor, Kimberley Raunikar, 1959-
    The intentional family : celebrating adoption / Kimberley Raunikar Taylor.
        p. cm.
    Includes bibliographical references.
    ISBN-13: 978-0-8341-2313-7 (pbk.)
    ISBN-10: 0-8341-2313-4 (pbk.)
  1. Adoption—Religious aspects—Christianity. 2. Adoptive parents—United
States—Biography. 3. Intercountry adoption—United States—Case studies. 4.
Intercountry adoption—Romania—Case studies. I. Title.
    HV875.5.T39 2007
    362.734092—dc22
    [B]
                                                                    2007004706

10 9 8 7 6 5 4 3 2 1

CONTENTS

ACKNOWLEDGMENTS

First, I give praise and thanks to my Lord and Savior for the precious gift of my son, Valentin.

To my loving and devoted husband, Daniel; words can never fully express my heartfelt appreciation for your desire to become a father to the fatherless and a husband to the widow.

To Sue Jones; I greatly appreciate the talent you shared while helping to lay the foundation for this project.

To my parents; I am especially grateful for your unconditional love for my son, and for the many hours of babysitting provided while I labored over this book.

To my Joy of Living Bible Study Group at Second Baptist Church in Houston; I am grateful for your genuine prayers and support during my life trials and triumphs.

To the Goldstons; thank you for modeling true friendship during the adoption of Valentin and the loss of my husband.

To Andrea, Karen, Sharie, and Denise; thank you for your suggestions and encouragement during the review of my original manuscript.

To the Bauers, Driscolls, Droddys, Rines, Scotts, and Stulps; may your efforts be blessed for taking the less traveled road with adoption.

To Nicoleta, the mother who gave my son unforeseen opportunity by letting go of him; I pray for your salvation and peace of mind.

And, to the late Don Raunikar; I am eternally grateful for his willingness to become an adoptive parent.

+ CHAPTER 1 +

ADOPTION IS IMPORTANT
TO THE HEART OF GOD

IN JANUARY 2004, I GRIPPED THE HAND OF MY adopted 4-year-old as we stared at the open casket containing the lifeless body of my husband. I attempted to sort through the many questions my son expressed about his father's sudden and untimely death. The questions were justified, yet I could not provide a good answer for: "Why did Jesus want Daddy in heaven instead of being with me?" I had known this man for almost 14 years, but my son had known him only two and a half years. So many questions were left unanswered, his and my own.

If it were not for my strong faith and trust in God, I may have faltered in my faith during this sudden change of season in my life. In those early days of widowhood I knew great grief, but I also knew that God was with me and He had not failed me. I believed without a doubt that God continued to hold a plan and a purpose for my life. He had always been there working, teaching, and encouraging me along the way no matter how difficult life had become. However, this new turn of events was peculiar and unexpected, and with greater and more severe consequences. It was no longer just me; I now had a young son depending on me for his every need.

Weeks after the funeral, my mind began racing with thoughts: *Did God really want us to adopt this child that is now, once again, without a father? Did I really hear God's voice when He said to me, "This is your son"?*

However, when I reflected back to the months before the adoption, I was reminded of the spectacular promise God made to me.

For years our marriage was filled with infertility treatments, turmoil, and indecision as my husband and I struggled with the ability to have a child. A few weeks after we finally submitted an application to an adoption agency, I felt an unusual presence of the Lord's Spirit as if a warm blanket were being wrapped around me. The date was February 14, 2000. The details of that day are written in my journal as I described the growing impression that somehow February 14 would be significant in the life of our baby. God spoke to me quietly and clearly, even providing a scripture that I declared in writing as "God's promise to our baby":

> "But Zion said, 'The LORD has forsaken me, and the Lord has forgotten me.' Can a woman forget her nursing child, and have no compassion on the son of her womb? Even these may forget; but, I will not forget you. Behold I have inscribed you on the palms of my hands" (Isa. 49:14-16).

Seven months later I received a phone call from the social worker at our adoption agency. My husband and I had been matched with a baby boy in Romania. She described photos of a child with fat, chubby little legs and a charming smile. Eager to give me as much information as possible, she began to describe the baby's medical history and background.

"But what about February 14?" I asked. "Is there any pertinent information that relates to February 14?"

"No . . . no, I don't see anything here," she said.

"Well then, what is his name?" I asked.

Because the records were hard to read and written entirely in Romanian, the social worker began to spell out the baby's name: "V–A–L–E–N–T–I–N."

We both gasped. The baby's name was Valentin. God had confirmed His promise. He had not forgotten us—not me, and not Valentin.

The changing face of adoption

As few as 30 years ago, stating that you were adopting a child was a phrase uttered in the privacy of family, and not words prospective parents proudly proclaimed to a public audience. There existed a negative stigma associated with adoption; some people believed children being adopted were "bad seeds" having been rejected and abandoned by someone "bad" who did something "bad." These false judgments drove the element of secrecy prevalent among the closed adoptions of the past. Thankfully, attitudes toward adoption are changing and becoming more positive, possibly because of more awareness and personal exposure. A survey performed in 1997 found that six in ten Americans have experienced adoption personally, meaning that they, family members, or close friends either were adopted, had adopted a child, or had placed a child for adoption.[1]

It is comforting to know God's heart has a special place for adopted children. Did you know, as Christians, we are God's adopted children? God actually gives His children the wealth and rights of royalty! In Galatians and in John, we are identified as children of the King with rights to God's inheritance.

> "In order that He might redeem those who were under the law, that we might receive the adoption as sons" (Gal. 4:5).

> "But as many as received Him, to them He gave the right to become children of God, even to those who believe in His name" (John 1:12).

Adoption inheritance

In the Roman Empire, adoption was a cultural custom for a man (or couple) without children to provide him with an heir. The adopted child's relationship to the new family was, for all intents and purposes, the same as what existed between a father and natural child. Also, if a relative died leaving orphaned children, a family member usually adopted the children. Today we would call this a "related adoption." The 2000 U.S. census recorded that related adoptions, initiated mainly by stepparents, make up about 40 percent of all domestic adoptions.[2]

As with the Romans, the formal process of adoption in our culture assumes there will be a transfer of inheritance to the adopted child. For us as Christians, not only a monetary transfer but also a spiritual transfer of inheritance takes place. My son, Valentin, will have the opportunity to benefit from the many blessings of his new family's heritage. Christians experience this same type of benefit when we are adopted into God's kingdom. We have access to the mind of Christ for godly wisdom. We can count on God's character and integrity to strengthen us and help us make the right choices. We trust in God's protection. The following verses in Romans reflect our adoption inheritance as Christians:

"For you have not received a spirit of slavery leading to fear again, but you have received a spirit of adoption as sons by which we cry out, 'Abba! Father!'" (Rom. 8:15).

"The Spirit Himself bears witness with our spirit that we are children of God" (Rom. 8:16).

"And if children, heirs also, heirs of God and fellow heirs with Christ, if indeed we suffer with Him in order that we may also be glorified with Him" (Rom. 8:17).

"And not only this, but also we ourselves, having the first fruits of the Spirit, even we ourselves groan within ourselves, waiting eagerly for our adoption as sons, the redemption of our body" (Rom. 8:23).

Transfer to new life

When God adopts us, we move from hopelessness into a future filled with hope. This is exactly what an orphan encounters with human parents. My son was living in a country with an ungodly heritage and economic poverty. He had no parents to claim him and to help him grow in truth and righteousness. His future was full of dead ends and despair. He owned nothing as an orphan, neither the clothes on his back, nor a comb or brush; he was destitute.

Valentin discovered many unique challenges during his transfer to a new life. He had to learn not only a new language but also things we take for granted, such as the requirement of sitting securely in a highchair or car seat. In the early months of adjustment, he believed these new contraptions were confining, keeping him from experiencing his new world to the fullest. He rebelled greatly against his new culture and principles for safe living. As he adjusted and matured, he was more able to understand that the contraptions he at first believed were confining actually provided him safety and security in a harsh and unfamiliar world. Likewise, as we embark on our Christian journeys, we experience similar adjustments. When we start to understand God's character and His desire to protect us, we begin to soften and accept His principles for living. Little by little, we let go of our old rebellious nature and learn to obey Him.

Our God and Creator knows what it means to take on the challenges of adopted children with a hopeless past. He chose to take on that challenge to save us from our previous life set toward destruction. Despite our disobedience, our Lord demonstrates His love for us. And daily, our Blessed Father models His love through His gifts of grace and forgiveness so that we can share in the eternal rewards of heaven, our inheritance.

Grafting and adoption unions

"But if some of the branches were broken off, and you, being a wild olive, were grafted in among them and became partaker with them of the rich root of the olive tree, do not be arrogant toward the branches; but if you are arrogant, remember that it is not you who supports the root, but the root supports you. You will say then, Branches were broken off so that I might be grafted in" (Rom. 11:17-19).

Comparing the horticultural technique of grafting with adoption provides an interesting perspective for adoptive parenting. The rootstock (or family) and the scion (or adopted child) both inherit value and diversity when a successful union is formed.

One interesting person, grafted into the lineage of Jesus Christ, is the biblical woman Ruth. She was born in a foreign land and taught to worship idols, but she and her sister-in-law married into a Jewish family living in her native country of Moab. When she became a widow at a young age, Ruth left Moab and followed her mother-in-law, Naomi, out of loyalty and love for Naomi and her God.

> "Then she said, 'Behold, your sister-in-law has gone back to her people and her gods; return after your sister-in-law.' But Ruth said, 'Do not urge me to leave you or turn back from following you; for where you go, I will go, and where you lodge, I will lodge. Your people shall be my people, and your God, my God. Where you die, I will die, and there I will be buried. Thus may the LORD do to me, and worse, if anything but death parts you and me.' When she saw that she was determined to go with her, she said no more to her" (Ruth 1:15-18).

Because of her obedience to God, Ruth found favor with Boaz, an Israelite, and married him. Their family line extended to Joseph, the husband of Mary and father of Jesus. As unusual as it may seem, an idol-worshipping Moabitess was grafted into the lineage of Christ, providing a rich and diverse heritage for our Lord.

On farms, grafting is commonly used to repair existing fruit trees. During a drought or a bad storm, a lemon tree may become damaged and in need of restoration. A trained farmer can take a pruned, young, healthy branch from a different tree (such as an orange or grapefruit tree) and create a grafted union on the healthy rootstock of the lemon tree.

Adoption brings new life to both sides of the union. It not only provides a desperate and disconnected child with a family but also provides a family with a child to nurture and care for. Like the lemon tree in need of repair, the new adoption union provides the opportunity for the couple to be fruitful for the first time or once again. And it gives new life and hope for the child to develop and mature into the man or woman that God intended.

God's amazing love transcends race, bloodlines, and cultural differences. He places more emphasis on creating loving families that will worship and serve Him than on maintaining perfect bloodlines. He made that clear when He removed His chosen race (the Jews) from the rootstock, and grafted the Gentiles in their place. Romans 9:8 tells us, "It is not the children of the flesh who are children of God, but the children of the promise are regarded as descendants."

Ensure an adoption success

As I pursued adoption, I began to understand that not all children experience permanence in their initial placements with a family. Well-meaning parents attempt to commit to their newly adopted child, but something goes wrong during the initial bonding period, causing them to reach a hopeless state of dissolution with the child. I do not want to judge these parents because I do not know their hearts or personal struggles and, statistically, the older the child at the time of adoption, the higher the probability for disruption to occur.

What is disruption? According to the National Adoption Information Clearinghouse (NAIC), the term "disruption" is used to describe an adoption process that halts before legalization, resulting in the child returning to foster care and/or to another set of adoptive parent(s).[3] It also is reported that disruption and dissolution can occur after adoption; however, the probability rate for occurrence is low.[4] And reports reflect that with proper education and preparation, the potential for disruption or dissolution is greatly minimized. According to the NAIC:

+ Most adoptions do not disrupt before legalization; more than 80 percent remain intact.[5]

+ Most adoptions do not dissolve; more than 98 percent are not terminated after legalization.[6]

+ Less than 0.1 percent of adoptions are contested each year.[7]

+ Adoption disruption and dissolution rates have remained relatively consistent over the past fifteen years, ranging between 10 and 20 percent depending on the type of adoption.[8]

+ Less than 1 percent of infant adoptions disrupt.[9]

+ 10 to 12 percent of adoptions of children ages three and older disrupt.[10]

+ For children placed for adoption between ages six and twelve, the disruption rate is 9.7 percent.[11]

+ For children placed for adoption between ages twelve and eighteen, the disruption rate is 13.5 percent.[12]
+ For children of any age with special needs placed for adoption, the disruption rate is 14.3 percent.[13]
+ Placements of older children and children with histories of previous placements and longer stays in the foster care system are more likely to disrupt.[14]

Like the strong root system necessary for grafting, an adoption should begin with a couple deeply rooted in their faith. During growing season, the farmer must prepare the rootstock, used to support the graft, with substantial cultivation, watering, and nurturing in order for the transplant to be successful. It is equally important for a couple to prepare for adoption through cultivating knowledge, understanding, and wisdom with which to raise an adopted child. This preparation and planning will help to ensure a permanent placement.

In the same way, an unsuccessful graft is similar to an interrupted or failed adoption. Unsuccessful tree grafts primarily occur when the rootstock does not quickly form a strong union with the grafted branch. This failed graft most likely resulted from poor preparation for the union, or it might have been a result of not having the adequate physical support needed to bond the two entities together. In addition, it might not have been carefully nurtured and protected against natural enemies during the early days and weeks while the union was forming. When a successful union is prevented or disruption occurs, the branch is forced to create its own energy to produce growth rather than benefiting from the rootstock's plentiful nutrients. Without the proper flow of water and nutrients, the grafted branch will eventually wither and die.

In adoption, there also are enemies hiding and waiting to pounce on the vulnerable new relationship. Preconceived notions from outside skeptics with a "doom and gloom" prognosis can initiate adoption failure. Also, the child's own experience with abandonment and isolation will no doubt generate feelings of fear and confusion during this delicate time. A good bond or union in an adoptive family depends greatly on the emotional and spiritual sturdiness of the family and extended family to demonstrate their acceptance of the new child. Just as with a fragile grafting, for a child to thrive and grow emotionally and spiritually, he must receive a constant flow of love, faith, prayer, and loving understanding.

The power of the family to heal or wound, to include or exclude, to build up or destroy, has a critical and lasting effect on an adopted child. Before that child can say, as Ruth did, "Your people are my people," the family members must demonstrate that she is their child forever. It is critical that a strong family support system provides unconditional love to reinforce the new union with the adopted child. This provides the feeling of security the child needs to believe she is in a safe and secure place.

Parental responsibility

Even though an adopted child will inherit many positive attributes from his new family, including a Christian heritage, this does not automatically translate to the child inheriting salvation. As the book of Romans tells us, we inherit our standing as children of God through believing in Jesus Christ as our Lord and Savior. Our birthrights and adoption certificates only sanctify us. It is the obligation and responsibility of the husband and wife to raise their children in a community of believers and teach them God's Word in order to establish a foundation for a relationship with Jesus Christ.

I also have met wonderful single Christian men and women who have sacrificially and successfully adopted and fostered children in need from around the world. These men and women are pouring their lives into these children and teaching them about Jesus Christ. After all, isn't this God's desire for the orphaned?

"Religion that is pure and undefiled before God, the Father, is this: to care for orphans and widows in their distress, and to keep oneself unstained by the world" (James 1:27).

Though single parents do not have the support of a spouse, they have a tremendous support through their covenant relationship with Christ and through the body of Christ, or fellowship with other believers in the church.

Because of this community, there is no need to fear or feel hopeless as difficulties manifest within the lives of our adopted children. One of the great blessings of our Christianity is that our adopted children will benefit from the blessings of our covenant relationship with God. With God working through us as parents, these children can transcend their difficult beginnings and walk in the abundant life God intended.

I Was Not There

I was not there
When you were knitted by His hands,
When He shielded you
And protected you from the world's plan.
When you groped for your first breath,
I didn't hear your cry.

I was not there
To know your hunger,
To wipe your tears
Or squeeze you tight.
And what about those long nights
As you listened for the footsteps
And the turn of the knob,
Waiting for the next nurse to spot your eyes.

I was not there
For your first dimply smile,
Or your first steps that made you fall.
Or your first tooth
When it pained through your gums.
Who was there to praise you
Or hand you a ball?
No, I was not there, but God was.
He captured those moments
For all of eternity
And whispered to you sweet love.

No, I was not there
To love and boast
Of God's beautiful gift.
But God was there! The One we trust
And the One who loves you the most!
—Kimberley Raunikar Taylor

+ CHAPTER 2 +

ADOPTION: A QUICK FIX
OR A LOVING SACRIFICE?

UPON ARRIVING IN BUCHAREST, ROMANIA, THE DAY before I was to meet my son, the reality of my decision to adopt hit me head on. After our Romanian translators identified my family from our photographs, they excitedly embraced us and escorted us to a van outside the airport. As we loaded our luggage, we were approached by two young and shabbily dressed Romanian boys, probably about ten and twelve. Boldly, they walked up to my father and in perfect English asked him for money. My father reached into his pocket and pulled out a wad of cash, handing it to the oldest boy. They nodded to him and quickly moved on down the street. As we were driving away from the scene, one of the translators said they were street boys without parents who lived by scavenging for money and food. At night they would sleep with other homeless street children like themselves, deep underground in the sewer system of Bucharest.

I choked back the tears as I realized exactly what my purpose was for this trip. I was rescuing my child from eventually being homeless, from living without loving parents, from sleeping in the dark, cold and dirty sewers. It deeply pained me to realize there are many more children all over Romania who had not and would not escape this destiny. Over the next few weeks we would encounter many street children desperate for money, who needed loving families to show Christ to them. In downtown Bucharest, I squeezed my small son tightly to my chest as another homeless boy carrying a baby approached us. They were both dirty and hungry and, again, the boy spoke perfect English requesting milk money for his baby sister. It was disturbing to see the horrific circumstances in which these children were trying to survive. As we crossed the street, I kissed my son and whispered God's promises to him.

"The angel of the LORD encamps around those who fear Him, And rescues them" (Ps. 34:7).

Adoption: antidote or blessing?

Choosing to adopt is not a decision to take lightly. I have heard some people naively say that adoption is an easy way to produce a family without all the pain. This is far from the truth. Adoption, generally birthed in pain and loss, gives rise to complex issues for which some people are not adequately prepared. A child put up for adoption at any age, including infancy, bears the mark of rejection. His wounded heart harbors difficulties for the child and the adoptive parents. Through the years, both must learn how to manage and cope with the wound. Some adopted children manifest minimal pain, but others struggle greatly with who they are and where they came from. More so than biological parents, adoptive parents need to be prepared to persevere in helping their children overcome the challenges that arise from their harsh beginning.

Each adopted baby and child has a unique past. Adopted children can be compared to a foreigner living in a foreign land. We need to welcome our new blessing into our home while embracing her cultural differences and uniqueness. They need to believe we accept them for who they are, not for what we need them to become. It is not an easy task to incorporate a stranger into an existing family. Older adopted children will be unfamiliar with the values, customs, culture, and religious beliefs of their new families. Perseverance coupled with strong boundaries will befriend parents trying to help a traumatized child adjust to yet another set of circumstances.

Check your motives

Answering the question, "Why do you want to adopt?" is as crucial as answering the question, "Why do you want to marry this person?" Just like marriage, adoption can be entered into with the wrong motives and expectations, causing undue hardships. Adoption must be approached with much prayer and consultation. Ask the Lord to open the eyes to your heart so you may see clearly what is in your heart in regard to adoption.

Self-centered hearts do not make for prospective adoptive parents. Paul warns us against not putting others' needs above our own: "Do nothing from selfishness or empty conceit, but with humility of mind let each of you regard one another as more important than himself; do not merely look out for your own personal interests, but also for the interests of others" (Phil. 2:3-4).

As you proceed in the adoption process, ask God to confirm that you have made the right choice. My husband and I sought adoption with caution, excitement, and inquisition by checking and double-checking our hearts' motives. Proverbs 16:9 tells us that, "The mind of man plans his way, But the LORD directs his steps." Is the Lord guiding your steps, or are you forcing the decision to adopt? Sound wisdom and discernment come from the Lord. God's wisdom protects us because He knows what is best for us. The book of Proverbs cautions us about stepping out in a course of action without first seeking sound wisdom: "My son, let them not depart from your sight; Keep sound wisdom and discretion, so they will be life to your soul, and adornment to your neck. Then you will walk in your way securely, and your foot will not stumble" (Prov. 3:21-23).

Being satisfied with our adoption choice means we view parenting as a privilege rather than a God-given right. Whether we adopt an infant or older child, our pure motives will help us demonstrate unconditional love and acceptance to our children. With pure motives, we can learn to work with the gifts and talents inherent to each child, and develop these gifts using creative means.

Be careful of entering into adoption out of feeling sorry for a child. This situation can foster a codependent relationship with the child instead of one where nurturing and respectful love exists for one another. Codependent parent-child relationships can foster all kinds of problems in the future that are unhealthy for both sides.

Infertility is the most common reason people turn to adoption. However, infertility is not the only reason Americans choose to adopt. Some people want to provide love and nurturing to orphans who would otherwise go parentless. They want to extend God's love, comfort, and gift of salvation to those who would otherwise live in darkness without witnessing the true character of God.

From infertility to adoption

Why do Americans pursue infertility treatment before adoption? According to the NAIC, the adoption process is initially viewed by many infertile couples as time-consuming, intrusive, and beyond the couple's control. Couples who give birth as a result of donor insemination choose the procedure primarily because of their dissatisfaction with the adoption process on three counts: long waiting lists; grueling and demeaning selection process; and worries about adoption laws and the security of adoptions.[1]

However, the NAIC also reports that people who decide to adopt do so for many reasons and, ironically, infertility is one of the most common motivating factors. Of those adoptive families who have experienced infertility, approximately half of those with fertility problems undergo medical treatment for an average of three years prior to adopting.[2] In one study, more than 80 percent of parents adopting independently or through a private agency said that their inability to have a biological child was the reason they chose to adopt.[3] By contrast, only half of those adopting from foster care cited infertility as the reason for their decision.[4] As studies and trends indicate, when the hope of fertility has run its course in a marriage, adoption becomes a popular option.

My spouse is not on the same page

I believe God transitioned me from the hope of a biological child to the possibility of adoption long before my husband. By the age of 36, I was diagnosed with infertility and began undergoing infertility treatment. This lasted until I was 40 and proclaimed to my husband my weariness with continuing treatment. Grief overcame him quickly and with great intensity. He suddenly realized that his dreams of fathering a baby were most likely not going to happen.

After considering adoption for quite some time, the Holy Spirit began to reaffirm that I could love an adopted child, but my husband still needed time. Joseph, the adoptive father of Jesus, had at least nine months of preparation before the birth of his nonbiological son. After the angel Gabriel visited him, Joseph's heart must have needed time to reconcile the fact that he would be raising a child that was not of his own body. We do not know for sure how long this process took him (maybe five minutes, five days, or five months), but we do know that he embraced Jesus as if He were his own. By taking his son to the temple for naming, circumcision, and dedication, he made a public statement demonstrating his parental responsibility as father to Jesus. We witness this act again, 12 years later, when Joseph painstakingly spent several days searching the city for his lost child. Also, by teaching Jesus the only trade he knew, carpentry, he was transferring his legacy to his oldest son.

Today, prospective adoptive parents do not have the divine help of the angel Gabriel to encourage us in our pending parenthood of a nonbiological child. But we do have the divine power of the Holy Spirit comforting and working in our behalf.

How do I pray for my spouse?

I learned that the cultivation of my husband's heart was best left to the power of the Holy Spirit. My badgering and strong, convincing cases were like hard pulsating hailstones compared to the gentle and encouraging whispers of the Holy Spirit. After God had been working on my heart for some time, I began to implement the following steps into my prayer requests so as to not pressure my husband with the prospect of adoption that he was not ready to accept.

1) For a grieving spouse:

Sometimes a spouse can get stuck in the anger cycle of grief, but not because of infertility. The death of a parent or a loved one, the loss of a job, childhood trauma, or marital dissatisfaction can keep someone stuck in grief. If your spouse is showing signs of anger, pray for God to reveal the source. Then ask God to heal his pain and hurt. Pray for him to not blame God or others, and share with him the blessings of infertility you have experienced.

If your spouse is still grieving over the loss of a biological child, then your spouse must resolve this dilemma before taking the steps toward adoption. The time it takes to reconcile this in his heart is out of your control. Release this problem to God and pray for your spouse. Like He did with Joseph, God will help your spouse resolve the grief on his own personal timetable.

If you believe your spouse is stuck in the denial stage of grief, ask the Lord to begin moving him from the "ideal" solution to a "real" solution. Adoption is a "real" option that can be pursued while remaining hopeful for a biological child. I believe this is where God changes people's hearts, opening them to the idea of adoption while also providing hope for the truly hopeless. Once I started to pray this way, my husband moved very quickly through grief and on toward acceptance of adoption.

2) For an indifferent spouse:

Some spouses are indifferent to their partner's desire to pursue adoption. These partners need a different type of prayer. The indifference a spouse has in the early stages of adoption can lead to a lack of support in the later stages of the process. Adoption is not a process where one spouse can carry the leadership and burden alone. The other spouse will eventually need to take a supportive and dual leadership role in persevering through this lifelong commitment. The partner of this type of spouse should:

1. Pray that God would lead you both to be united in one spirit toward a common goal.

2. Pray that God will touch your spouse's heart and change the indifference to that of a passionate desire for God's will.

3) For a reluctant spouse:

It was the Holy Spirit, not me, that changed my husband's heart regarding becoming an adoptive parent. My role was minimal. I solicited prayer support from my church prayer group and asked the Holy Spirit to work on his heart to bring about the will of the Father regarding adoption. It is imperative that a couple pray together and ask the Lord to guide both of them through the process of discerning whether adoption is the right path.

If your spouse lacks understanding or knowledge of adoption, then with your spouse's agreement, invite a family for dinner that has an adopted child. Have the parents talk through their own adoption decision and how they worked through any reluctance of becoming an adoptive parent. Then ask your spouse to read some information about adoption. Or suggest that the two of you attend an adoption orientation meeting. It is important to not overwhelm your spouse with too much information at this stage. Keep the information limited, general, and upbeat without strings attached.

As you begin praying for your spouse, it may be difficult to wait for God to move and answer your requests. Believe and have faith that God will provide an answer to your unique situation. Leave the burden with God. By giving up control of your situation and by placing the resolution in God's hands, a peace will come that surpasses all human understanding.

A baby at my age?

We are never too old to choose God's best for our lives, or to be a part of God's plan. When we are on the outside of a situation looking at all the negatives and the positives of a decision, we can easily become overwhelmed. From our limited human perspective, we can be deceived into believing our age, physical limitations, and circumstances cannot be overcome by God. However, God is not limited to operating within our human restrictions. He proved this several times with older first-time parents in the Bible and continues to prove it today. Here is what one adoptive mother believes:

"I adopted my daughter, Katie, from China when she was only nine months old, and I was 47 and single. A case of middle-aged insanity? Not on your life! The moment I held her in my arms I knew Someone Really Big had brought us together."[5]

While contemplating adoption at the age of 40, I was concerned my age presented problems for raising a child. I considered possible midlife health problems and diseases that could cause debilitation. I thought about being a senior citizen as my child entered the difficult teenage years. These are all real issues and should not be ignored. However, knowing God directed me to adopt a baby at 41, I have no doubt He will provide all that is needed to carry His work to completion. And He will not abandon me halfway into the plan. Psalm 16:11 says: "Thou wilt make known to me the path of life; In Thy presence is fullness of joy; In Thy right hand there are pleasures forever." Who would have imagined, but Sarah was 90 when God chose to fulfill her heart's desire to be a mother. I believe we are never too old to be a part of God's plan of having children, whether biological or adopted. Even after the death of my husband, God continues to provide me with an overabundance of blessings with which to raise my son, and as His Word proclaims, God longs to be gracious to His children (Isa. 30:18).

Faith versus fear

One Sunday afternoon several months after my son arrived from Romania, he woke from a nap screaming as if sheer terror was gripping his little soul. My husband and I were in the next room counseling a young couple about their impending marriage commitment when his screams startled us. I leapt from the couch and ran into his room less than 20 feet away from our den. I wrapped him in my arms and tried to console him with words of affirmation. But it only made his screams worse. Nothing comforted his condition. It wasn't until I began to pray and asked God for His help that Valentin finally began to quiet. My husband and the young couple joined with me to pray and asked for God to intervene for this child. To this day I cannot explain the fear and confusion that overcame Valentin that eerie Sunday afternoon; however, I do know that God heard our prayers and intervened to calm his terrorized soul.

Many people have spoken to me of their great reluctance to adopt. Some believe the potential issues associated with an adopted child are overwhelmingly complicated. Some have known friends and family members with an adopted "problem" child. Strong Christian men and women have confessed to me their lack of belief in their own abilities to cope with the challenges adoption brings into a family. I, too, had experienced, and sometimes even now experience, these same fears of inadequacy. However, throughout my adoption journey, God continues to remove the doubt these fears create. Below are some verses the Lord gave me to address my fear:

+ Admit your fears. Confess them with humility. "The LORD upholds all those who fall and lifts all who are bowed down" (Ps. 145:14).

+ Don't focus on the fear; focus on God. "I sought the LORD, and he answered me; he delivered me from all my fears" (Ps. 34:4).

+ Put your hope in Christ and in His ability, not in your own limitations. "But the eyes of the LORD are on those who fear him, on those whose hope is in his unfailing love" (Ps. 33:18).

God regularly teaches me through various trials to trust in Him, giving me the strength to work through concerns and issues regarding little Valentin. And as God shows me He is the source of all knowledge, wisdom, and strength, I am coming to the understanding that I am powerless in my own strength. Just like the Israelites during their time in the desert, my responsibility is to humbly submit to His commands and let His power work through me to provide the success He desires.

When we reject fearful messages, embrace God's truth and believe in His faithfulness and trustworthiness, we are empowered to do what God has intended for us from the beginning. Adoption is not a mountain to climb; it is a daily adventure, bringing incredible eternal blessings affecting generations to come. The experience can bless everyone it touches. But we must enter into this relationship with our eyes wide open, carefully weighing the good with the not so good.

Mother's Day

I am afraid
To plant this seed.
The sun is warm,
The earth is rich and ready,
But the days go by, and still no planting.
Why?

The springtime of my life
Is passing too.
And ten years' planting
In a willing soil
Have borne no living fruit,
So many times I've waited,
Hoped,
Believed,
That God and nature
Would perform
A miracle
Incredible but common
Nothing grew.
And often times I feel
The mystery of life and growth
Is known to all but me,
Or that reality
Is not as it appears to be.

I have a choice:
To put aside this seed,
Leaving the planting
To the proven growers,
Pretending not to care

For gardening,
And knowing
If I do not try I cannot fail.

Or plant,
And risk again
The well-known pain
Of watching
For the first brave green
And seeing only
Barren ground.

He also spoke
About a seed,
The mustard's tiny grain,
Almost too small to see,
But, oh—the possibilities!
Those who doubt,
Who fear,
Are not inclined to cultivate it.
But it was to them He spoke,

And God remembered Sarah . . .
Rachel . . .
Hannah . . .
Elizabeth . . .

The seed is in my hand,
The trowel in the other;
I am going to the garden
And the Gardener,
Once more.
— Margaret Munk[6]

+ CHAPTER 3 +

DECISIONS:
THE HEART OF THE MATTER

GROWING UP IN THE '60S, I LIVED A SHELTERED
life—a two-parent household in a moderate-income neigh-
borhood in Houston, Texas. At that point in my life, Cau-
casian, English-speaking people were the extent of my
small world. However, I had a fascination with children
from other countries and cultures. Pursuing this interest
was limited to what I could find in books and movies. Like
most little girls, I enjoyed stories about knights and prin-
cesses. I gave my dolls European names and imagined they
lived within the majestic gardens of beautiful castles.

It was sometime during this impressionable time in my
life that God quietly planted a seed of desire in me to adopt
a foreign child. I cannot explain this desire logically, for I
did not know anyone adopted from a foreign country. But
unknown to me, God already was at work preparing the
way for my future adoption encounter. Thirty years later, I
could no longer ignore God's gentle prodding. When the
pain of my infertility became a reality, I began to pursue
those early dreams and desires. With the approval and sup-

port of my husband, I embarked on the journey of uncovering the fascinating world of adoption, step-by-step and book-by-book.

"Trust in the LORD, and do good; Dwell in the land and cultivate faithfulness. Delight yourself in the LORD, and He will give you the desires of your heart" (Ps. 37:3-4).

Baby, toddler, or special needs?

An estimated 37 million orphans live in today's world.[1] This vast spectrum provides us with many possible options. One of the first steps in the adoption process is deciding what type of child you desire to parent. Do you want a newborn, infant, toddler, school-aged, or older child? Do you wish to adopt within your race or from another race? If from another race, do you have a preference? What about from a different country? Do you desire a child who has special needs? Do you have a gender preference? Would you be willing to adopt twins or a sibling group?

If you do not have ready-made answers for these questions, one way to decide is to read books written about personal adoption stories. *Loved by Choice* by Susan Horner and Kelly Fordyce Martindale[2] covers a variety of different types of adoption possibilities and provides great insight into each of these decisions. In addition, talk with other adoptive parents about how they made their decisions. No perfect formula or process exists to help you identify your specific desires. Sometimes the answers you uncover don't have any logic behind them; it might just be an impression or feeling you have, and this is OK.

Every couple adopting has a unique situation in which to provide for a child. The National Council for Adoption defines "special needs child" in this manner:

"This usually refers to children who are considered 'hard to place' and the definition depends on the state. Almost all states include nonwhite children in the definition, although the children may be healthy infants. . . . In addition, most states include children who are older (usually beyond toddlers), children who are members of sibling groups (some families find it difficult to manage two or more new family members simultaneously); children with physical, emotional, or mental handicaps."[3]

One of the most startling statistics from the 2000 Census is that one in every eight adopted children has a disability[4] ranging from cleft palates to spina bifida. My husband had muscular dystrophy, confining him to a wheelchair, and his disability discouraged us from taking on the added responsibility of a handicapped or emotionally disabled child; however, many special needs children are readily available for a loving family eager for the challenge. The 2000 Census report also shows that about one in six adopted children (17 percent) are a different race than the head of their household,[5] and about half (49 percent) of foreign-born adopted children come from Asia.[6]

Domestic or international?

The next important decision is whether to adopt a child from the United States (domestic) or one outside the country (international). Statistically, the greatest factor in choosing international adoption is the age of the adoptive couple. Many domestic adoption agencies have imposed age limits for couples wanting to adopt. Over-40 couples are usually put into a higher-risk category along with couples who have a disability or health issue.

Recently, more agencies have become able to facilitate either domestic or international adoption, however, it is important that you decide between the two options as soon as possible. The aspects of each type should be thoroughly examined and weighed before a decision is made.

Domestic adoption

According to the National Council of Adoption, domestic adoption generally fits into three categories: public agency or child welfare system (40 percent), private agency (30 percent), or independently by individuals (30 percent).[7] All types require a home study and have legal requirements dictated by a state governmental agency. The legalities of a domestic adoption are more predictable and reliable than in foreign adoptions. Due to standardized requirements across state lines, illegal baby trafficking is less likely to occur domestically than in less regulated foreign countries.

The welfare system, through foster care programs, provides the opportunity for public domestic adoption. Within this system, the couple has time to monitor and test their compatibility with a child before a formal adoption is pursued. About 126,000 children with an average age of roughly 8 years are in the U.S. foster care system and eligible for adoption, says Thomas Atwood, president of the National Council for Adoption.[8]

Adopting domestically has many advantages. Generally speaking, a domestic adoption involves less culture shock for parents and children. Plus, newborn infants only a few hours or days old are available. If medical issues arise and medical history is needed, the birth parents of a child adopted domestically can be easier to track. Within the United States, the birth mother is more likely to receive good prenatal care, resulting in a healthier baby. The travel expense required to deliver the child to his new home is minimal compared to the expenses required to travel overseas. The INS does not get involved; passports and dossiers are not required; there is no U.S. embassy or foreign government hassle; and less paperwork in general is needed to process the adoption.

Today, the vast majority of domestic adoptions are open to some extent, as opposed to the traditionally closed adoptions of the past. An open adoption is one with mutually disclosed personal information about birthparents and adoptive parents. In a typical closed adoption, no personal or identifying information is exchanged between the parties. In this case, the agency or attorney acts as the mediator, protecting the identity of its clients from each side of the adoption. Prospective adoptive parents can find the idea of open adoption frightening. Some couples are fearful about becoming too closely involved with the birth mother, believing she might have more influence in the life of their child than desired. However, varying degrees of an open adoption can be decided during preadoption interviews and counseling sessions. A couple should not agree to an arrangement with which they are not comfortable.

One of the downsides of domestic adoption is that it is easier for a birth mother to initiate procedures to reclaim her child. This decision can devastate an adoptive family after having waited so long for a baby, only to have their hopes dashed after months of bonding and attaching.

With the increasing number of American couples desiring to adopt infants, the demand now greatly outweighs the supply, so much so that the power of choice in domestic adoption has transitioned from the adoptive family to the birth mother. Young, impressionable, and highly emotional young women between the ages of 13 and 21 are typically in control of who will gain the right to take custody of their unborn children.

One friend told me of her approach in finding and adopting two children. She and her husband mailed letters to friends and family stating their interest in adopting a baby and soliciting their help. Within six months, they received information about a young pregnant mother unable to care for her baby. Both of their adoptions were initiated based on the association of various friends with a qualified adoption attorney completing the process.

International adoption

Although foreign adoptions receive a lot of attention these days, they represent less than 15 percent of adoptions in the 2000 Census.[9] The largest percentage of international adoptions are finalized by childless couples with infertility problems over the age of 34. As previously noted, age is a major factor for couples deciding to adopt internationally.[10] Most international countries do not impose age limits for adoptive couples.

In the last 10 to 15 years, couples have aggressively sought international adoption as a way to circumvent the extensive waiting period typically associated with domestic adoption. The time from application to adoption varies greatly for international children, but you can expect six to nine months as the minimum and up to two years being the maximum wait. Many variables can cause delays. One is misdiagnosed children who are actually more severely handicapped than originally thought, causing some potential parents to pass over the child and restart the matching process. Another is that the foreign government involved may change its requirements midstream, or a child may unexpectedly become unadoptable due to birth parents and relatives reentering the picture. And sometimes a sibling surfaces, further complicating the original decision of the couple to adopt only one child.

International adoption most often provides a closed adoption environment with anonymity for the adoptive parents and birth parents. This is appealing to many Americans; however, very young infants are more difficult to adopt. Due to the limits inherent to most foreign government processing, babies do not become adoptable outside their country until six to nine months of age. In most countries, before a child is legally available for adoption, relatives and residents must first formally surrender parental rights to the government. By the time these steps are completed, several months have elapsed in the life of a child. The baby is sometimes six months old or older before he or she actually enters the system and is available for adoption outside the country. Add to this the additional time it takes to process a foreign adoption, and the baby usually is at least 12 to 15 months old before adoptive parents can bring the child home. However, there are exceptions, and foreign adoption processes constantly change and improve. Asian countries such as Vietnam have been known to provide infants in international adoption situations, and some of these babies have arrived home as young as three months old.

Private agency adoptions

People who choose private agency adoptions do so primarily because private agencies can provide a range of options and helpful associations that are normally not available in independent adoption situations. Good agencies are designed to facilitate an adoption union using careful guidance and counsel to all parties involved. They employ, through contract and/or permanent employment, licensed professionals trained to counsel prospective adoptive parents as well as birth mothers about their adoption decision. They arrange a home study and assist with meeting the agency and state requirements. Some agencies require training as a prerequisite to the adoption as well as assigned reading and support group encounters. Their guidance and support can be invaluable in positioning a couple for a solid match with a child.

Every agency has its own qualification requirements for prospective adoptive parents. However, a few requirements are mandated by each state's government: being at least 18 years of age; having state residency for a certain length of time (varies by state); and proving the ability to provide a safe and stable environment in which to parent and nurture a child. Most nonmandatory requirements are quite negotiable with the agency. For example, the upper age limit used by most agencies is 40 years separating the child and the adoptive parents, although exceptions may be made if the prospective parents are considered active and healthy. (Interestingly, many foreign countries regard age and maturity as sought-after virtues in prospective adoptive parents, rather than as an obstacle to the adoption.)

The ability to pay the costs and fees that will be associated with your adoption is of significant importance. But, if needed, there are organizations that provide adoption loans and grants. And I've seen many parents find creative means to obtain the money for extra expenses through fund-raising dinners, community yard sales, church raffles, and such.

Certain criminal convictions of the prospective adoptive parents or others living in the home may prevent an adoption being approved. Prior legal or criminal matters, problems with child abuse, financial instability, or substance abuse are all issues to be taken under advisement with the agency before a background check is performed. Depending on the circumstances involved and the agency's flexibility in its decision, waivers can be issued on a case-by-case situation.

While selecting an agency, look for one with a philosophy and mission that fits your personal and family values. This will help ensure the agency becomes your advocate. You want its employees to fully understand your needs, desires, and limitations. Unfortunately, some agencies will take your money, place you on a waiting list, never place a child with you, and never provide you with an acceptable explanation. By selecting an agency that clearly supports you, they will utilize your precious time to your best advantage. We chose our agency for the following reasons:

+ It was well known and established in its field
+ It had a good reputation for maintaining honesty and integrity

+ We liked the people in the office who were assisting us
+ It had the same religious affiliation
+ It had overseen several international adoption options
+ The office was a short drive from our home
+ The personnel demonstrated a willingness to work with my husband's disability
+ The personnel demonstrated real concern for our desired timetable

Since we were clear about our objectives and thoroughly researched our options, Buckner International Adoption Agency in Dallas, Texas, was an obvious choice. I encourage prospective adoptive parents to talk to newly adoptive parents living near them and find out what they liked and did not like about their agency. Use these conversations to decide what is important to you. After selecting an agency, talk to agency staff and administrators over the phone or in person, and attend an orientation meeting. After you have met resident social workers and addressed your concerns with administrators, you will have a good idea how your case will be handled.

It is also important to remember that during the highly emotional course of adoption, situations will arise where you will feel tension and frustration with your agency. Remember that this is normal. Whenever people, relationships, and a high degree of emotion are involved, both parties at some point in the process will fall short in their ability to be diplomatic and sensitive to each other's needs. Many times the adoption agency has little control on the other side of the transaction. We must be careful to not lay blame where blame is not due.

On the other hand, if you feel your agency is not being honest with you and you cannot get truthful answers, it may be time to cut loose and look for another agency that you can better communicate and work with. The money you may forfeit early in the process is insignificant to the problems and unnecessary expenses you may encounter later with a deceptive agency.

Pursuing adoption when a parent is disabled

How does someone with a disability proceed with the decision to adopt? We did not let my husband's disability deter us in the least. At the time of our application, my husband had no known complications from his disability that prevented him from living a healthy life, and his doctor issued him a positive medical evaluation. When we approached our agency about our decision to adopt, we wanted to know from them from the start if they believed my husband's disability would prevent us from adopting a healthy baby internationally. The director was candid with us and said she did not believe it would be a major deterrent. However, they added, depending on the country from which we chose to adopt, the agency would need to initiate contact with its officials to screen our disability issue before we invested too much time and energy in the process.

In our application process, we approached the disability in a positive manner. We clipped magazine pictures of parents in wheelchairs with their children and families, and we found articles about disabled adoptive parents. These articles demonstrated how parents with limited mobility could attach, love, care for, and discipline their children using creative means.

The cost of adoption

According to the new census, 2 million adopted children live in the United States.[11] Statistics reveal that their parents are typically older, better educated, and have more personal wealth.[12] Private adoption is known to be pricey; however, the bottom line is that adoption costs vary. With the help of a public child welfare system, a domestic adoption can cost as little as $500, where a private international adoption can be as high as $35,000.[13] The wide variation depends upon the circumstances and the type of adoption.

Agency fees are usually the largest percentage of the cost associated with a private agency domestic adoption. Public or governmental welfare agencies generally are less expensive. Independent adoptions by individuals include not only legal fees but also, in some states, birth mother living expenses and medical costs. Below are examples of the fees involved with an independent adoption by individuals:

+ Attorney fees
+ Court filing costs
+ Home study fees

+ Guardian *ad litem* fees
+ Adoption consultant fees
+ Birth mother's living expenses (depending on the state)
+ Medical, counseling, and hospital expenses for birth mother
+ Travel expenses for out-of-state birth mothers
+ Advertising costs

An agency or attorney can provide an estimate of anticipated expenses. To help offset these costs, a Federal Adoption Tax Credit[14] is available for expenses related to the adoption of a child. Children with special needs, internationally adopted children, year of the adoption, and the number of children adopted are items considered in the calculation of the tax credit.[15]

Generally, international adoptions cost the most but vary across agencies and the countries from which children are adopted. International adoptions may include but are not limited to the following costs:

+ Agency fees
+ Home study fees
+ INS fees
+ Passport and document fees
+ International government fees
+ Dossier preparation fees
+ Orphanage fees
+ Translator fees

+ International travel expenses (flight, hotel, meals, transportation, gifts, communication, etc.)
+ Medical evaluation expenses (for child)
+ Other processing fees

International adoption costs also are subject to the whims of the foreign government involved. The Romanian Council on Adoption delayed our adoption because of an unusual request: that we have our dossier authenticated by the State Department in Washington, D.C. Since our agency had never dealt with this request from Romania, they proceeded through the tedious and lengthy process with caution. This last-minute request is one example of unanticipated expenses and delays that can occur in the adoption process.

In the end, our adoption process extended months beyond the original estimated timetable. The process stretched our faith, our pocketbooks, and our patience. However, I would recommend international adoption to anyone up to an adventure and a new challenge. The reward of my son finally coming from the other side of the world to live in our home made all the difficulty worthwhile.

Happy endings

Our friends Harry and Katherine desperately wanted children, and with the hope of a biological child gone, they decided to investigate adoption. And so it was, this childless couple began the pursuit of adoption. Within the next four years, God led them to adopt two toddlers from different regions within Russia. This couple is now blessed with a beautiful little boy and girl who sing Bible songs and laugh and play like all happy and well-adjusted children. The journey they began in their late 30s and mid-40s was a long one, taking them through the unknown depths of infertility and through a wonderful adventure of a life they could not have anticipated.

Our friends Marie Elena and Kevin and their five adopted children inspired our own adoption decision. We became a regular part of their family as we watched their adoption story unfold. In their mid- to late 30s, God led them to adopt five babies in six years. One adoption was through an independent association, two were domestic through a private agency, and the last two were international adoptions from Vietnam. Even though adoption was not in their initial plans, both of these couples believe that God led them to adopt each one of their children.

Our personal adoption choice

Very soon after we arrived at an international adoption orientation meeting provided by Buckner, the agency representative handed out booklets containing pictures of children available for adoption in Russia. We listened to the speaker as she explained the fate of these young children. We could see the sadness and fear in their eyes from their photographs. Our hearts went out to them.

Two sets of adoptive parents and their children were

brought into the room to tell their adoption stories. One of the couples was about our age and had gone to Russia three months earlier to bring home a 12-year-old girl. Her mother had died in the hospital two years earlier, leaving her an orphan in the care of the Russian government.

Weeks before they were to leave for Russia, the Russian government identified an 8-year-old sister within its orphan system. The youngest girl had been separated from her sister two years earlier due to a diagnosis of mental retardation. Russia's general policy is to not split sibling groups, so the couple was asked if they wanted to take both girls. They excitedly and graciously agreed.

When they arrived at the orphanage where the youngest girl was located, the couple quickly picked up on the missed medical diagnosis. She was thin and frail, but she was also bright and happy. After more questions and inquiries to the caretakers, they concluded the girl was malnourished rather than mentally handicapped. Within a few weeks, the couple returned to Houston, Texas, with two happy and reunited sisters. All of their lives were changed forever, and for the better!

The second family was an older couple who already had raised two boys who were away at college, but they believed they had more years of parenting to offer someone in need of a family. A situation arose for them to adopt a 14-year-old Russian girl, who would soon be released to the streets, as was typical for 16-year-old orphans. We were told at the orientation that a large percentage of the Russian orphans who are released to the streets die within a few years. The couple took compassion on her and went to Russia to bring her home to the states where a more hopeful life could be provided. Within a few months, the young girl was happily settled into American life.

These stories gave us hope and ignited a passion for adoption in us. We discovered foreign adoption could be a positive experience for us while also meeting the needs of helpless children. After the meeting, my husband and I waited for the agency director to come to our table to meet with us. She encouraged us to pursue the adoption process further and said we were invited to call her anytime with questions. Before we left the meeting that night, my husband leaned over to me and whispered the sweetest sign of all that he had been hooked: "Well, I guess we will have to remodel our upstairs to accommodate three or four adopted children." I remember smiling to myself and thinking, "Thank you, God. My husband's grieving is over." When I reported the transformation of my husband's heart to my church prayer group the next week, they rejoiced with me at the awesome work of God!

As we left the orientation that night, my husband provided me with more insight into his struggles with adoption. He said he had always believed that most couples' primary motive for adoption was to fill the love hole in their hearts. He believed most couples were adopting from the perspective of, "How can this child meet my needs?" instead of, "How can I best help an orphan in need?" My husband truly believed that parenthood should be a sacrificial choice instead of a selfish one. When I understood the motives of his heart, I better understood his original reluctance to pursue adoption.

"Greater love has no one than this, that one lay down his life for his friends" (John 15:13).

Our home study was conducted in April 2000, and we were asked to finalize our choice of international country by June. We were struggling between Romania and Russia, but when Russia shut down its international adoption program on June 1, 2000, to modify procedures and guidelines, our decision became clear. These changes would require recertification by all adoption agencies, and our agency was no exception. Buckner advised us that it might be six months or more before its Russian adoption process would again be operational. We believed this was our answer to prayer, and we chose Romania as our adoptive country.

Trust God, not people!

After my husband and I prayed and decided on a country, we sensed much peace in believing we had made not only the best choice, but also the right choice. However, as we began to tell friends and relatives our choice, we experienced varying degrees of responses. For some, the mention of Romania conjures up dreadful images of thousands of abandoned babies lying in orphanage beds, left uncared for and starving to death. Thanks to our national media in the early '90s, this is the image most Americans have of Romania's orphan system.

One doctor scowled at the mention of a Romanian adoption. His comments on our adoption choice were quite defeating, even though he had never been to Romania, nor did he know personally about its orphanages. This comment from a professional, respected medical doctor could have destroyed my confidence in our choice of Romania, but I held fast to what I believed was God's choice for us. As I began to research Romania through travel books, I began to see the same message again and again: "Americans, beware of traveling in Romania! It is not safe to be on the streets by yourself. Pickpockets are everywhere and the police are unsympathetic." This news is enough to keep anyone from traveling to Romania! However, the negative press did not frighten me enough to cause me to change my mind. We chose to stay on God's track and continue to pursue His plan even when the world around us was not always showing us support.

"For the LORD gives wisdom, and from his mouth come knowledge and understanding. He holds victory in store for the upright, He is a shield to those whose walk is blameless" (Prov. 2:6-7).

+ CHAPTER 4 +

INSTANT TODDLER, INSTANT SHOCK:
PREPARING TO ABSORB THE SHOCK

"A mother is born the moment she feels the
love in her heart for a child she has never seen."[1]
A Love Like No Other, by Elisa Morgan

IN THE YEAR 2000, AS I PROCEEDED THROUGH THE
formal process of adoption, I began to have many questions
and concerns about my ability to love a child who was not
my biological child. My heart was skeptical as well-meaning friends and family expressed to me that it was a
woman's natural desire and God-given instinct to be able to
love any child. Parents with biological babies have nine
months of natural reminders—for mothers, every minute
of every day—that a baby will soon change their lives forever. Adoptive parents do not have this initial physical connection, causing us to rely on other means to prepare us for
child-bonding and parenthood.

Adoptive parents especially need preparation. Instant
parenthood with a toddler or adolescent can be shocking to
anyone. We need to adapt our expectations to accept the
challenges and experiences awaiting us in raising an adopted child. Daily prayer became my initial link to my child,

and God used my emotional and spiritual journey to develop in me a heart like His, helping to prepare me for the trials of parenting my toddler.

Fruits of the Spirit

Obsessing about the impending responsibilities of parenthood can overwhelm us. Parents need a godly standard after which to model their behavior. Without one, it is easy to follow the well-meaning but greatly deficient worldly standards. In our humanness, as we attempt to reach for the godly standard of parenthood, we will fall short of our goal. However, through God's redeeming forgiveness, love, and grace, we can always start again. Isaiah 30:18 says, "His mercies are new every morning!"

The term "fruit of the Spirit" is found in Gal. 5, where the writer tells us that as we live in the Spirit and begin to walk in the Spirit of God, we will exhibit these fruits in our lives: love, joy, peace, patience, kindness, goodness, faithfulness, gentleness, and self-control. As a mother of a preschooler, I find it more difficult to walk in the Spirit now than I have at any other time in my Christian life. It seems my character is tested when I am sleep deprived, achy, and most vulnerable to anger. At these times, the only way my character can exemplify the fruits of the Spirit is with the Holy Spirit's help. And I know I need Him now more than I've ever needed Him before.

Galatians 5:24 says to crucify the flesh with its passions and desires. We must trust God that He will help us deny ourselves and let the Spirit of God empower us to be the selfless parents we need to be. I try to pray regularly that these godly traits become manifested in my daily life. I will never fully perfect these attributes while living on earth, but God desires that I die to my sinful nature and attempt to develop godly character in all I say and do. Truly, this is a challenge in raising any active preschooler.

A quiet heart

Mary, mother of Jesus, is a wonderful example to us of a quiet heart. Mary did not ask many questions of the angel Gabriel when he came proclaiming her virgin pregnancy. She took God at His Word. She did not let fear or unbelief enter her life to fester and cause unfaithfulness to God's plan.

> "And Mary said, 'Behold, the bondslave of the Lord; be it done to me according to your word.' And the Angel departed from her" (Luke 1:38).

She obeyed God's call on her life and was quick to be faithful. After Jesus' birth and upon the visit of the shepherds who had been visited by the angel of the Lord, God's plan was confirmed to her through other people.

> "And all who heard it wondered at the things which were told them by the shepherds. But Mary treasured up all these things, pondering them in her heart" (Luke 2:18-19).

Even when Mary did not understand the remarks from the temple priests regarding her son, she remained quiet and did not overdramatize or cause unnecessary fear to manifest within her family.

"And they did not understand the statement which He had made to them. And He went down with them, and came to Nazareth; and He continued in subjection to them; and His mother treasured all these things in her heart" (Luke 2:50-51).

Elisabeth Elliot says that in her opinion, a believer "keeping a quiet heart" is the meaning of life. She describes how at Wheaton College, in 1947, she wrote a few lines of a prayer about this desire:

"Lord, give me a quiet heart
That does not ask to understand,
But confident steps forward in
The darkness guided by Thy hand.[2]"

She goes on to say, "This was my heart's desire then. It is the same today. A willing acceptance of all that God assigns and a glad surrender of all that I am and have constitute the key to receiving the gift of a quiet heart. Whenever I have balked, the quietness goes. It is restored, and life immeasurably simplified, when I have trusted and obeyed. God loves us with an everlasting love. He is unutterably merciful and kind, and sees to it that not a day passes without the opportunity for new and applications of the old truth of becoming a child of God. This, to me, sums up the meaning of life."[3]

I believe it is important to add that a quiet heart is not passive. A quiet heart asks for the Holy Spirit to act. Mary was not passive when the angel revealed God's plan at the time of her immaculate conception. She believed, and her belief was not passive. Her prayer explains her strong belief and faithfulness to God:

> "And Mary said: 'My soul exalts the Lord, and my spirit has rejoiced in God my Savior. For He has had regard for the humble state of His bondslave; for behold, from this time on all generations will count me blessed. For the Mighty One has done great things for me; and holy is His name. And his mercy is upon generation after generation toward those who fear him. He has done mighty deeds with His arm; He has scattered those who were proud in the thoughts of their heart. He has brought down rulers from their thrones, and has exalted those who were humble. He has filled the hungry with good things; and sent away the rich empty-handed. He has given help to Israel His servant, in remembrance of His mercy, as He spoke to our fathers, to Abraham and his offspring forever.'" (Luke 1:46-55)

In my heart I knew God was up to something "big" concerning our adoption. The only people with whom I shared the intimate correspondence God was having with me were close family and intimate friends. Anyone else would not have understood my revelations. I attempted to do what Mary did, keep a quiet heart, and ponder the things God had told me. Even when people around me were questioning the agency and governmental delays and preparing me for the worst, I knew in my heart that God would be faithful to His promise.

A long-suffering heart

Mary and Joseph spent their lives enduring the worldly consequences of Mary's immaculate conception. Most people in their hometown must have strongly questioned their story. They must have endured harsh gossip, rumors, and whispers centering on the baby's birth and life. I speculate it was difficult for them to watch their oldest child be taunted and teased for His unnatural wisdom and abilities. And no one can truly know the suffering Mary endured as she watched Him be rejected and tortured by His own people and put to death in a criminal manner. At Jesus' circumcision, Simeon spoke of Jesus' destined future and Mary's suffering by saying, "A sword shall pierce your soul." I believe Mary and Joseph knew what long-suffering was all about.

A teachable heart

Mary and Joseph were willing to be changed and molded by God's will for their lives and believed God's plan for them, even though it did not line up with their own human reasoning. As we let the world's system of beliefs be incorporated into our daily lives, deception can slowly creep in without our having full understanding and awareness of its happening. It takes the power of the Holy Spirit moving and working in our lives to reveal these wrong thoughts by the renewing of our minds.

One way God revealed deception in my life was through a fund-raiser I operated before we adopted our son. During the time of our home study, I discovered an organization through our agency that was collecting shoes for orphans. These shoes would be collected around the state and ultimately shipped to orphanages in Russia, Romania, and China for special delivery. I decided to set up collection sites around our city and advertise the need for orphans abroad to have new shoes for the winter months.

Over the next few months, many people were willing to collect shoes and deliver them to my collection sites. We had specifically stated in our careful advertising that we needed new or "slightly worn" shoes. The overseas governments were known to reject used clothing and shoes in the past, and we did not want our efforts to be in vain.

As we began to collect the shoes, I began to notice different types of "givers" to the needs of the orphans. Many graciously went to a children's department store and paid full price for brand-new shoes. Sometimes shoes were bought on sale at bargain super centers, and sometimes "almost new" shoes that were hardly worn were deposited.

Another group gave money to cover shipment of the shoes. These groups were by far the most generous and thoughtful of the givers.

However, to my dismay, the most prevalent type of givers were people who cleaned out their children's closets and brought to the collection site very torn, dirty, and worn-out shoes. These orphans already had torn, dirty, worn-out shoes. They needed new, comfortable, warm shoes. I was probably more sensitive to this because my soon-to-be child would be in the group of children receiving these shoes. These gifts now had personal meaning to me, and I wanted the best for all of these children.

I began to think back over the years of the various donations I had given to our local mission and considered my own motives. I was surprised at how often I, too, had been more interested in disposing of old clothes and things of no use to me than putting myself in the place of the people in need. I don't ever remember thinking of the mission as a place where people go for comfort, love, and support and not just for clothes and food. God showed me that the condition of my clothes, linens, and food were a sign of love and compassion from my family to our local community in desperate need. The people coming to be clothed and fed had old, dirty, and tattered clothes and shoes to wear. People who enter the mission doors for help have nowhere else to turn. They go to the mission in search of help from caring people, not to receive other people's old discards.

What did my box of rejected, tattered, and worn clothes say to those lost souls and suffering individuals? Was I communicating to them that I was giving them what I thought they deserved? Was I saying that I would not eat outdated cans of tuna on my pantry shelf, but they could? Did I believe that they should be grateful for what they could get? Was I saying by my gift that because they were in need, it was OK to give them substandard provisions? My heart began to grieve because of my thoughtlessness and selfishness concerning my past gifts of charity. I assumed that because I was giving I was fulfilling a need. I did not consider the underlying message I was sending to my local mission. I never thought about how someone would feel to take off a torn and faded shirt only to put on a duplicate of a different color. How I confessed my thoughtlessness to God! I then thanked Him that He was changing my heart. He was purging my false beliefs and misunderstandings and replacing them with new understanding and sensitivity to the needs of others. This new adjustment in my attitude was preparing me to look at my impending parenthood with purer motives.

A heart of sacrifice and obedience

When the angel Gabriel approached Mary and Joseph concerning God's plan for their lives, their reaction was one of sacrifice and obedience. They made a choice to believe God's promise. As parents, we need to believe that with God, all things are possible (Matt. 19:26, Mark 9:23, Mark 10:2).

When we lack faith, we allow fear to entertain our thoughts, and desperation will drive us to make poor choices.

A parent who continually thinks of his family members and puts their needs before his own is a sacrificial parent. These are the attributes we want to model to our children so they will pass them down to their children. As I have begun to raise my son and learn to discipline and teach him, I have come face-to-face with my pride. When I am in public and my son acts out in disobedience, I have learned to let go of my pride and accept the fact that my son often will be unable to display in public the good behavior that I know he is capable of performing. Outsiders do not know about his background and emotional issues and do not always administer patience and understanding to his inappropriate behavior. I have learned to apologize gracefully when we have offended others by his enraged outbursts and tantrums in restaurants or grocery stores. Becoming angry and resentful at the lack of others' understanding is not the response God wants from me. James 4:6 says, "But He gives a greater grace. Therefore it says, 'God is opposed to the proud, but gives grace to the humble.'"

A parent with an obedient heart is able to be responsive to a child and spouse's needs, but humility must come before obedience can be sacrificial. A humble heart has the capability to be sensitive to the needs of others.

"If therefore there is any encouragement in Christ, if there is any consolation of love, if there is any fellowship of the Spirit, if any affection and compassion, make my joy complete by being of the same mind, maintaining the same love, united in spirit, intent on one purpose. Do nothing from selfishness or empty conceit, but with humility of mind let each of you regard one another as more important than himself; do not merely look out for your own personal interests, but also for the interests of others. Have this attitude in yourselves which was also in Christ Jesus, who, although He existed in the form of God, did not regard equality with God a thing to be grasped, but emptied Himself, taking the form of a bond-servant, and being made in the likeness of men. And being found in appearance as a man, He humbled Himself by becoming obedient to the point of death, even death on a cross. Therefore also God highly exalted Him, and bestowed on Him the name which is above every name" (Phil. 2:1-9).

Jesus Christ reflects His sacrificial character by showing us His perfect obedience to the Father. We will never perfectly perform on our own merits, but through the power of the Holy Spirit, we can believe the best in people, love the unlovable, sacrifice the unsacrificable, and become humble in our obedience.

According to Gen. 8:21, "Sacrifices are a soothing aroma to the LORD." He is greatly aware of all the sacrifices we make, small and large in nature. Our acts of gratefulness and servanthood do not go unnoticed to the most important One in our lives. Our families may not notice, give us credit, or respond to our giving hearts, but God is always watching.

My heart develops

As I studied with my Bible study group at church, 1 Cor. 4:1 was addressed in one of our weekly sessions: "Let a man regard us in this manner as servants of Christ and stewards of the mysteries of God." I pondered that verse during my study time and did not have an answer as to how it applied to me.

As I met with my small group of women the next morning, I still did not have an answer to the question regarding the explanation of the mysteries of God. I sat down in the circle of women and prayed for God's leading in His Spirit. We were deep into the lesson when the question came up, and the other women were equally puzzled. However, in an instant, God's Spirit spoke to me and revealed my answer, saying, "During this delay I'm developing in you a mother's heart." Wow! This was incredible.

It had been a great mystery as to why God was allowing this adoption to take so long. It seemed to me that our baby would be better off with us, his new adoptive parents in the states, than in a third world country where there was no hope for him. After that day, when people asked me why the adoption process was taking so long, I had an answer. It was not an answer with excuses directed toward the Romanian government, but an answer given to me personally—God was using the drawn-out period to prepare me for parenthood. And today, even though my child is safe at home, God isn't finished with me. He continues to develop my heart through His great grace and mercy on my life.

+ CHAPTER 5 +

THREE OF HEARTS:
MOVING FROM DESPAIR
TO THE JOY OF ADOPTION

My Child Was Born Today

My child was born today.
While another woman felt the wonder of her birth,
My heart longed to see her face.
Far away across the sea
She nurses at her mother's breast,
A woman who loves her as I do.
Yet the harshness of this woman's fate
Brings motherhood to me.
Her family broken, mine begins.
Oh, who can understand the ways of life
When loss and love join hands?

Angela McGuire

East Lansing Michigan

Perspectives on a Grafted Tree, by Patricia Irwin Johnston[1]

Reflecting back to the days of our fertility treatments, I especially remember a bright sunny morning in late March 1999. I had been to the infertility doctor the day before and had been given an injection to stimulate ovulation. He told me tomorrow was the day for us to perform our fifth artificial insemination. I had briefly turned on the television the morning of the insemination while I was ironing my blouse. One of the commentators from a national network morning show was saying, "If you want assurance to know you can have a millennium baby, today is the last day to conceive." I thought at the time, "Wouldn't it be nice to have a millennium baby!" I smiled to myself and quietly mentioned to God that I wanted a millennium baby.

The Bible says, "God's compassions never fail and are new every morning" (Lam. 3:22-23). That day, God answered my meek little request, but not in the way I was thinking. On the other side of the world, in a foreign culture, a young, unmarried, helpless girl became pregnant. It was this conception that God would use to bless me as I lived two continents away in Houston, Texas.

On the morning of January 1, 2000, I distinctly remember waking and feeling an incredible peace and joy deep within in my soul. On that very special day, I sensed something marvelous and wonderful was happening in the world. Even the Y2K scares seemed insignificant to the quiet peace I felt that day. It was weeks before the adoption application was submitted, and I had no reason to believe my thoughts and internal joy related to what God was doing in a small town in Romania.

However, a young, frightened girl had been driven in the cold and snow to the town's only hospital located a short distance from her apartment. She was in labor with a baby she knew she would not keep. Her plan, supposedly encouraged by her shamed parents, was to stay in the hospital until she had recovered enough to leave and return home. So after six days of recovery, she walked out of the hospital without the baby boy she brought into the world on New Year's Day.

God's confirmation of our match

Months came and went as we waited for each new step in the adoption process to be completed. I held tightly and firmly to God's promise about little Valentin. Other people around me were becoming skeptical that the baby would ever be brought to Houston, but deep down I knew what God had told me. I was holding firm to His promise.

After many months of waiting, well-meaning friends and relatives began trying to prepare me for the worst. Stories of how adoption agencies had misled helpless couples for months only to have their hopes destroyed were being whispered around me. But I knew what I knew. And when we received notice that our final court date in Bucharest had approved our adoption, I was elated with joy!

Two days later our travel plans had been coordinated with the Buckner translators in Tereg Mesus, Romania, and with the Romanian HUG foundation representatives in Bucharest, Romania. We received our expected travel dates and made our travel arrangements.

April 22, 2001

After arriving in Bucharest, we met for dinner with

the HUG Foundation representatives involved in the Romanian side of the adoption. They reserved a lavishly decorated banquet room for a cozy dinner. We ate "Romanian style" with multiple courses of food lasting late into the night. It was delightful to take our time eating and enjoying the new friends with whom we would spend the next week. Rika was the social worker in charge of placing Valentin with his foster parents. She was the only one present who actually knew him and the only one who could not speak English. The HUG representative, Vali, translated Rika's descriptions and comments regarding our son. She said he was handsome and smart.

Everyone was excited and greatly anticipating our meeting with Valentin the next day. Nicole, another HUG representative, explained the itinerary. We would be leaving in a van for Braila in the morning. Romy was our driver, and Dana and Nana were our official translators. Nicole and Vali would be remaining in Bucharest. To my great and wonderful surprise, Nicole said I could take Valentin with me tomorrow and keep him from this point of the trip on until we left the country. She said, "He is yours now." These words startled me as they shot through me. Reality was settling in that the most anticipated day of my life was imminent!

After dinner, in my hotel room, Nicole graciously handed me Valentin's papers reflecting the foreign adoption of our baby. WOW! *He is truly mine!*

The Significance in a Birth Name

Names as well as dates have always been significant to God. Many times in the Bible, God associated a man's name with a new beginning such as with Abraham and Paul. Proverbs 22:1 says, "A good name is to be desired more than great riches, favor is better than silver and gold." In her book, *Raising Adopted Children*, Lois Ruskai Melina suggests that selecting a child's name is particularly important for adoptive parents. It is a way to claim this child as their own and demonstrate to the child that he or she belongs to their family.[2] However, I also know that toddlers, unlike infants, have begun to personally identify with their name. We wanted to limit the number of unnecessary changes for our child. We believed he had enough traumatizing events behind and ahead of him. In addition, after discovering the significance of Valentin's birth name, I began to further question removing his Romanian name from the adoption papers. And I wondered if God might be showing me there was a need for us to preserve his birth name.

One day in September while working at the local bookstore, I shared my dilemma with a coworker. She immediately went to the baby section and pulled *Name That Baby* by Jane Bradshaw from the shelf.[3] In the introduction, Bradshaw explains how she derives the explanation and biblical support referenced for each name in her book. She explains how she first starts with the Bible to locate a biblical reference of the name. If one is not found in the Bible, she then goes to the language of origin by researching the many languages of the world. Once she finds a traditional meaning for the name, she locates a verse in the Bible holding that meaning, thought, or connotation. This is what I found in her definition for Valentin, a derivative of the name Valentine.

Valentin(e): To be Strong and Valiant[4]
"The Lord is my rock, . . . my fortress, . . . my deliverer; my God, my strength, in whom I trust" (Ps. 18:2).

Was God telling me that my son, Valentin, was to become a valiant warrior for His kingdom? Very possibly! I believed God was building a case to keep his birth name.

Addressing the birth mother's pain

Oklahoma, 1897

In 1897, my maternal great-grandmother was born to a poor farmer and his wife in a small rural community in southern Oklahoma. As the youngest of six, she experienced a hard and difficult life in a family with not enough food to eat or clothes and shoes to keep up with their adolescent growth. No one was surprised when she caught the eye of a young man from a neighboring town at the local dime store. At the tender age of sixteen, she thought a relationship with him would mean an escape from her difficult life. She became pregnant with his baby girl shortly after they met. He was young and immature and not willing to assume the responsibility of marrying and caring for a family. He had plans for his life that did not include additional unwanted baggage. Her parents arranged for the baby girl to be adopted by a wealthy doctor and his wife in a nearby town where the baby could be cared for properly and be legally given a father's family name. My great-grandmother could not bear the thought of giving her child to strangers, even though she was not prepared to emotionally or financially provide for the baby. Feeling humiliated and ashamed of her condition as an unmarried woman and unable to cope rationally, she abandoned her infant baby girl to her parents and ran away to the nearest city to escape the disgrace she felt. Her parents kept the child, believing she would someday come home to reclaim her.

Eventually, my great-grandmother did return to claim the child she had once abandoned. However, she returned pregnant and with her new husband, a Chickasaw Indian, who was living on a local reservation. Six months later, she delivered a boy, whom she loved and adored for as long as she lived. She eventually took parental responsibility for her daughter, my grandmother, but for the 65 years my grandmother lived, she said she was treated as an unwanted child by her mother. At a very young age, my grandmother's heart was filled with deep feelings of abandonment and rejection as she grew up in the shadow of her much-loved younger brother.

My grandmother followed in her mother's footsteps and became pregnant as a young teen. However, unlike her own birth father, this young man tried to assume his responsibility as a husband and a father, but the marriage ended shortly after the baby was born dead. She married again several years later and gave birth to my mother, her only living child. Years before she died, she expressed the sentiments wishing her mother had not been so headstrong against allowing her to be adopted by the family eager to take her as an infant.

Ironically, the day after my grandmother's death, the following letter to Ann Landers, a popular columnist of the day, was printed in *The Daily Oklahoman*.[5] A young woman's laments state her personal regrets about not following through with an adoption plan for her baby girl:

Dear Ann:

I've never written to you before, but the letter from the social worker hit me so hard I had to write. I want to say something to young unmarried mothers who think they should keep their babies "as a matter of pride."

I became pregnant at 16—unwed. Instead of thinking what would be best for the baby, I thought only of myself. I married the father. It was a disaster. We were divorced shortly after. I remarried and was again divorced. Between marriages I lived with family and friends. I never abused my child physically, but I never really loved her.

I have married again—at long last—happily, and we

have a beautiful baby. This time the bonding took place. Being a mother is a joyous, beautiful experience.

My first child is scarred because of the love I was unable to give her. Behavioral problems became so severe I finally had to send the child elsewhere to live. That poor little girl is torn between an emotionally dead past and a future without a firm basis.

Every day of my life, I regret not giving her up at birth. I deprived that child of the opportunity to be adopted by loving parents who could have given her the kind of love she deserved.

Name Withheld

Also City, Please

My mother found this page of the newspaper torn out and placed among her mother's personal items to be boxed and stored. We do not know who put it there, but the letter spoke the sentiments of my grandmother's heart, believing her life would have been less traumatizing if she had been adopted at birth into a loving family who wanted her and could provide a stable home life.

Romania, 1999

Valentin's Romanian grandparents remained conditioned from Ceausescu's rule that it was acceptable to abandon unwanted babies. His birth mother registered and signed in at the hospital on New Year's Day, knowing she would not walk out of the hospital with the baby she was carrying inside her womb. She must have experienced a similar "numbing effect" that western girls have when they decide to "not keep" their baby by aborting it. In both cases, the fate of the child is decided in an environment of shame, guilt, and fear. These feelings do not soon or easily go away just because the baby is done away with in secret.

I don't truly know the condition of her heart that day, but I thank the Lord she had the presence of mind and parental guidance to abandon my son at the hospital where professional caretakers were able to continue postnatal care for him. He was kept in the hospital for about four months until he was released to the baby orphanage, as is common procedure in Romania to keep abandoned infants until they reach a certain birth weight. This assures they will get the proper care and attention an infant requires.

Afterward, his birth mother returned to the apartment less than one mile away with her parents. Undoubtedly, the neighbors and immediate family were aware of the secret she tried to hide. She had not provided a name for the father or any identifying information about him. In fact, the only identifying information she gave the hospital about herself was her name and address. Her age, marital status, and medical history were not documented. She wanted to leave as little information as possible for future tracing of her indiscretion. Most unusually, she had left the hospital without signing away her parental rights, making Valentin ineligible for adoption. However, once he was old enough to go to the baby orphanage, the local police became involved to locate the birth mother and request her signature, which ultimately dissolved all of her parental rights. Her willingness to do this provided Valentin with more opportunities and hope than she ever could imagine.

October 2, 2000

We officially told Buckner we wanted to adopt Valentin. What a wonderful adventure we have in front of us. God has promised us this beautiful baby boy, and we are holding onto His promises as we wait for a court date in Romania. May God's Spirit move within the different groups responsible for making this all happen.

I pray Valentin's foster parents will take loving care of him. May the Lord meet his every physical, emotional, and spiritual need in Braila. I pray for his birth mother that she will respond to God's calling on her life and give her life to Jesus. Lord, please have mercy on her soul. May she find peace and rest in you.

Before I left the United States for Romania, I bought a Romanian New Testament Bible to give to his birth mother, believing I would locate her. But after telling a Buckner representative about trying to find and meet the birth mother, she discouraged me from trying to make personal contact. She said most mothers who sign over their parental rights do not know their baby will be adopted internationally.

Sometimes this new information causes them to question their initial decision.

My backup plan was to have someone deliver the Bible to her anonymously. However, after later discovering she moved from the only address I had and did not leave a forwarding one, I left her salvation in God's hands. I committed to pray for her over the years. Even today, I believe God has His hand on her.

During our weeklong stay in Braila, I located her parents' home address on a local map. I also found the address of the hospital where Valentin was born. I asked Rika to take me to where the birth mother once lived. I'm certain I was not the first adoptive mother to make such a request. She firmly stated that the young girl had moved away with her parents months earlier. She no longer could be found in Braila. However, it was important to me that I see her apartment. Our translators were sympathetic and talked to Rika about making the trip to the abandoned apartment. Reluctantly, Rika agreed to accommodate us.

April 27, 2001

Today Dana, my dad, and Rika and I went to the apartment building where Valentin's birth mother lived. It was the address on the hospital certificate. Rika told us she was a young, unwed mother of 21 who lived with her parents. They felt as though she had caused so much shame to the family that after the baby was born she left him at the hospital six days after delivery. A few months later, she moved with her parents to the countryside after selling the apartment. Dana and I walked inside the building and climbed the stairs to the top floor where her apartment was located. I wanted to take a picture of the apartment door. On the way up the flight of stairs a young man passed us. Dana asked him in Romanian if he knew the family who lived in apartment number 88. He said yes, he had known them, they were neighbors, but they had moved suddenly about six months ago. This helped to confirm our story from Rika. The apartment building was not for the indigent, and she most likely came from a respectable family.

Valentin's birth date is January 1, 2000. This makes him a turn of the century baby! He was born almost 2,000 years from when Christ was sent by our heavenly Father to earth. "God loved the world and gave His only Son so that the world would be saved and have eternal life" (John 3:16). What an incredible gift Jesus was to us. This arrival of Jesus was a surprise to most people, even though His coming should not have been a surprise. The Old Testament is full of prophecies declaring a king would be born of humble circumstances to come and save the people. Both Isaiah and David spoke of this king and foretold of his life and death. God prepares the righteous for his mighty works. He prepared Noah 600 years in advance before the flood came. Because of Noah's alertness to hear God and also because of his righteous living, his family was spared through the flood. The Book of Psalms says that the angel of the Lord encamps about the righteous (Ps. 24:7).

Even today we must be ready and alert to hear God's message to us. If I had not been alert on February 14, 2000, to hear God and to document His message to me, I would have missed God's blessing. I would not have heard His message and would not have the assurance and security in knowing Valentin was to be our son, and I would have gone through much unnecessary trial and anxiety over the problems encountered during the adoption process. Most importantly, I would not be able to share with others how God worked, promising to bring me my son.

+ CHAPTER 6 +

PREPARING FOR ADOPTION

IN THE OLD TESTAMENT, THE PROPHET ISAIAH PRO-
claimed that God told him to prepare the way for the Mes-
siah. "And it shall be said, 'Build up, build up, prepare the
way, remove every obstacle out of the way of My people"
(Isa. 57:14). Then about 500 years before Christ came to
earth, the prophets Malachi, Isaiah, and Zechariah all proclaimed that a messenger (John the Baptist) would be sent
to prepare for the coming of Christ. And Jesus told us almost 2,000 years ago that He would go to prepare a place
for us in Heaven (John 14:2). This is a lot of preparation!

Adoption also requires preparation. Long before my
husband and I began to consider adoption as an alternative
to biological children, God was preparing us for this future
event. He was moving in our hearts and clearing away obstacles so that we would be equipped to effectively parent
our child.

Prepare for a change in lifestyle

When a child arrives, whether he is an infant or a 5-
year-old, a new parent's personal time will be almost non-
existent. Throughout the transitional and adjustment phases

of the adoption, leisure mornings with coffee and devotional reading will be few and far between. Lunch dates with one's spouse or friends will greatly diminish because of new schedules and commitments involving planning and preparing meals, naptimes, and doctor appointments. Fitting in your personal shower and hygiene times will require daily strategy. And reading for entertainment will be replaced with analyzing instruction labels on cans of formula, medications, and toy assembly.

Children add a new dimension to the regular routine in our lives. They are curious about everything and want to touch, taste, and experience whatever they see as important to us. My son watched me put on makeup a few times before he asked for powder, lipstick, and mascara to be put on him. Then one day without my awareness, he quietly slid off the bathroom counter with a tube of my red lipstick tightly concealed in his little hand. He snuck over to the white sheer curtains in the master bedroom and began drawing on them. This creative decorating act rearranged my morning plans as I tried different techniques to remove the red lipstick from my curtains and him. I am learning to flow through these derailments with better ease and with a sense of humor; however, the number and volume of tasks I previously would have expected myself to accomplish in a day were limited the day my new son arrived. Today, if the basic and necessary daily tasks are accomplished, I've learned to accept that I have actually exceeded all reasonable expectations for the day. And most importantly, I know how grateful I am to have the blessing of Valentin.

Prepare emotionally and spiritually

My deceased husband and I often reflected upon the almost nine years we spent childless. We were both already 33 years old when we married, and according to medical professionals, we were biologically categorized as being "high-risk" for a pregnancy. We wanted children from the beginning, but unknowingly, we had a long road of preparation ahead.

My husband earned his doctorate degree when he was 31. He was essentially in school three-fourths of his life before we married. When most of the men his age were settling into a comfortable career and lifestyle, he was only just beginning his career-building process. Upon leaving my consulting job, my intentions were to help my husband build his private practice and to discover what God had planned for my life and our lives together. However, for the next five years, God took me through a period of healing in my life that I was not expecting. The emotional and spiritual development through which God led us in the beginning years of our marriage prepared our hearts to cultivate the fruits of the spirit needed for being unified in our path of parenthood.

God began to bring the most incredible godly older women into my life to pray for me, study with me, and guide me into a deeper understanding and commitment to Christ. He also brought to the surface childhood trauma that was keeping me in bondage to a life of legalism and pain. I did not know until then how much I did not trust God with my life. Nor did I know how angry with God I really was.

The initial trauma we fall victim to as innocent children is never our fault; however, the poor choices we make in the years succeeding the trauma becomes our road into bondage. The greatest preparation I did for our child was to find truth and peace in Jesus Christ and to be set free from the lies the enemy had fed me for so many years.

Get your house in order!

Ask God to show you the things in your life you will need to address before you are best prepared to bring a baby into your home. Solomon, son of King David, instructs us in Proverbs that before we set our plans in action, we are to consult with wise counsel (Prov. 20:18). Our marriages are always a good place to start in getting our house in order. You might be surprised at where God's preparation will lead you.

1) Pray together:

Pray together as a unified couple even if you have never done so before. If you are concerned that you do not know how to pray, remember that God knows your hearts and the Holy Spirit intercedes for us.

Most importantly, begin praying for your prospective child. Whether this child has or has not been conceived or is currently living in a difficult environment, he or she needs your prayer support. A special spiritual link will begin to develop between you, your spouse, and your child as you begin to pray.

2) Ensure healing from past marital offenses:

Couples can accumulate a lot of hurt and pain over the years in a marriage if they are not careful to keep short accounts of offenses. It may take the help and assistance of a professional counselor to help identify and work through serious issues. If harbored negative feelings exist, stressful times will trigger their release, preventing the Holy Spirit from interacting most effectively in our lives.

"Let all bitterness and wrath and anger and clamor and slander be put away from you, along with all malice. And be kind to one another, tender-hearted, forgiving each other, just as God in Christ also has forgiven you" (Eph. 4:31-32).

3) Develop better communication skills:

Learn to effectively listen and affirm each other. Deepen your understanding of your spouse's spiritual gifts, talents, and dreams. Effective listening skills are invaluable skills to parent your child.

Work at developing conflict resolution techniques. Unresolved conflict can close the doors to effective communication. Our children absorb what is modeled to them, and when effective communication is demonstrated, they will also become effective communicators. However, if conflict is left unresolved, listening skills are minimal, and anger and resentment are harbored, most likely they will learn to assimilate these same negative behaviors.

Develop structure in your daily living

To feel secure in their environment, babies and young children require daily routine and structure. Before our child arrived, my husband and I were very unstructured in our daily living. Our mealtimes were dictated by our fluctuating appointments, not by a daily routine.

In order to eliminate chaos and confusion, orphanages generally operate within highly structured schedules. And when our son arrived in Houston, in order to feel secure and safe, he craved his old familiar environment filled with rigid structure. Now we attribute some of his early anxiety to our inability to conform to a rigid structure quickly enough for him to feel the security he needed. I suggest to any prospective parent to begin engaging in a regular routine of daily good habits before your child arrives. Whether the child is coming from an institution or as an infant from the hospital, it is never too early to develop a plan for structure, something all children need to feel secure. Ultimately, when you are organized in your daily living, your child will feel more secure, and if you have not already done so, I've listed below some of the major areas in which to begin incorporating a structured routine.

+ Develop a morning routine with getting up in the morning, showering, getting dressed, and quiet time with God, as well as a nightly routine with winding down, preparing for the next day, and going to bed.
+ Develop regular breakfast, lunch, and dinner schedules. (Have four to five preplanned daily menus with ingredients on hand.)
+ Maintain a weekly grocery shopping schedule with an organized shopping list.
+ Develop a weekly schedule for housecleaning and laundry.
+ Develop a working system for organizing the paper-flow in your home. Have a central place for sorting and storing important mail, bills, and magazine subscriptions. At the same time, dispose of the clutter from junk mail and unnecessary paper that comes into the home daily. I found that by eliminating clutter, I eliminate confusion and chaos.

As you consider your own new daily routine, begin to visualize a child in your home and how you can best incorporate a morning and evening schedule to accommodate his or her needs. The schedule may change once the child actually arrives, but early planning and preparation will be helpful in establishing a routine.

Obtain prayer support from others

The Lord was my strength during our adoption process,

but my prayer partners became my support system. Knowing I had such special friends praying with me at every new step in the process gave me reassurance and encouragement. As changes developed during the adoption process and as the cross-Atlantic trip approached, I informed my support system of our changing prayer needs.

Pray for your future child

Most importantly, your child needs your prayer support. The prayers you offer your child now, even before you meet your child, will pave the way for his or her future relationship with Christ. Pray for your child's past, present, and future needs. I prayed for my child's protection and provision when he was still in the orphanage by asking God to guard his heart and mind against evil in his surroundings. I asked God to place a "hedge of protection" around and about him while he was in this delicate stage of developing and growing. And I asked the Lord to begin preparing him for the transition and adjustment into his new family.

We also prayed and asked God to heal any health issues he may have. We did not have a medical history profile on the birth mother and father of our son, so we prayed that God would be merciful to our child and prevent any genetic health disorder from surfacing into his life.

When you begin praying for your child, God will reveal your child's important needs.

Feb. 28, 2000

I pray for you that God will keep away the lions so they won't prey on the weak and young. May God place a hedge of protection about and around you, and may He be your shield and protection. May God keep fear from you (Ps. 91:13). I pray that when you lie down, you will not be afraid and that your sleep will be sweet (Prov. 3:24).

Learn about normal child development

When we understand the phases of development associated with normal children, we can better detect abnormal behaviors and developmental delays. Mary Hopkins-Best says, "Each stage of development is associated with certain cognitive, physical and social/emotional tasks which need to be accomplished before moving on to the next stage."[1] However, she also says, "Until you know your child, it is difficult to recognize unusual behaviors."[2] For initial preparation, we read books on child development, parenting, and discipline, and I talked to friends about any developmental problems they experienced. This information established a good foundation of knowledge and understanding, but the application of this information was more difficult.

Find a pediatrician

I interviewed pediatricians and found one I believed would work well with our family. Through his private practice, he had some experience with international children, and I saw this as an advantage. I sought his counsel on the kinds of food and milk I should take on the trip to Romania. Also, our adoption agency prepared us with information regarding the conditions in which the child would be living and how to help the transition go smoothly with caretakers, food, and clothing.

Cultivate adoptive and other parent relationships

As our home study was completed and approved, we were constantly educating ourselves about adopted children. We both talked to parents of internationally adopted children and discussed their experiences and daily life challenges. One of our friends with multiple adopted children was a vast resource of information. We talked for hours about her struggles in the adoption process, the children's adjustments, and her adjustments to each new child. Also, our agency provided names and phone numbers of recent adoptive parents for us to talk with.

Couples shared with us where they congregated at age-appropriate parks, playgrounds, restaurants, museums, and other toddler-friendly environments to facilitate learning and friendships. Being older parents, we did not have many friends with young children at home. So during our time of preparation, I began making efforts to develop friendships with older parents of young children in our church. I began seeking out those parents with adopted children as well because I wanted my son to develop some friendships with children of similar backgrounds. Later, these friendships were invaluable for sharing stories, parenting techniques, and prayer requests.

Learn about your child's heritage and culture

I checked out books from the library about Eastern European history, and gleaned as much as I could about the history and culture of the Romanian people. I studied old and current-day maps to understand the geography and war history so that I could gain more understanding about my son's biological family and ancestors. Someday my child will want to explore his native culture, and I want to be passionate about this discovery with him.

Gain knowledge about potential developmental problems

One of the most significant problems that can arise with an adopted child is the child's ability to successfully bond and attach with new parents. Dr. Gregory Keck, author of the very insightful book *Adopting the Hurt Child*, states that most professionals agree the first 18 to 36 months of a child's life are the most critical to developing healthy bonding and attachment to others.[3] He says that in a healthy bonding cycle, a child will learn that if he or she has a need, someone will gratify that need, where the gratification leads to the development of trust in others.[4] Failure for a bonding cycle to complete successfully will give way to lifelong implications for the child and those who are entrusted to his or her future care. Dr. Keck lists the developmental areas of greatest effect for children who have an interrupted bonding cycle:[5]

+ Social/behavioral development
+ Cognitive development
+ Emotional development
+ Cause-and-effect thinking
+ Conscience development
+ Reciprocal relationships
+ Parenting
+ Accepting responsibility

However serious these issues may manifest themselves in a child, Dr. Keck provides hope for the adoptive parent believing these problems can be overcome. He says:

"It is our firm belief that children hurt by abuse and neglect can learn to love and trust adults in a family setting. Growth and development continue throughout the life span, and it is rarely too late for a child to change. The better we understand what motivates these children, the better equipped we are to help them."[6]

Emotional issues

People who have raised, studied, or treated adopted children with emotional issues will all agree that similarities exist in their dysfunctional behavior patterns. In general, emotional disturbances are most commonly demonstrated through one or more of the following behaviors:

+ Fear of abandonment and rejection
+ Attachment issues
+ Separation anxiety
+ Grief
+ Guilt
+ Shame (lower self-esteem)
+ Lack of trust and sense of security
+ Difficulties with intimacy
+ Unexplained anxiety
+ Diminished social interaction
+ Depression
+ Poor impulse control
+ Aggression
+ Rage
+ Need to control
+ Lack of emotion or exaggerated emotion
+ Stealing and hoarding
+ Other generalized fears (e.g. loud noises, various textures)

Demonstrating rage and an extreme fear of rejection are very common behaviors in children who are grieving and experiencing attachment problems.[7] Attachment problems are typical for institutionalized children or any adopted child who has experienced neglectful and disrupted care.

Each of these issues can vary by child, and some adopted children do not experience these issues any more than a child who has never been separated from his birth mother.

Of course, other factors can aggravate these symptoms, such as an unstable homelife after the child is adopted, lack of acceptance from the family or extended adoptive family, or lack of understanding of these issues by the adoptive parents.

Developmental delays

Institutionalized children often experience mild to severe physical and emotional developmental delays. This can be partly because of the effect that abandonment has on the wounded heart of a child. However, developmental delays also may occur because of the following:

+ Lack of stimulation and touch
+ Crib confinement and restraints
+ Physical abuse
+ Sexual abuse
+ Neglect
+ Hyperactivity
+ Malnutrition
+ Mental retardation
+ Fetal alcohol syndrome

Developmental delays will become apparent in the life of a child when each new benchmark approaches in the areas of:

+ Sitting up
+ Crawling
+ Walking

+ Talking
+ Toilet training
+ Development of fine motor skills
+ Development of large motor skills
+ Cognitive abilities and problem solving
+ Learning

Deprived of early stimulation and nurture, a baby or child may not know how to calm himself or herself or to accept soothing from a nurturing parent, a coping skill normally learned in the first few months after birth.[8] We taught this skill to our son upon his arrival to our home. It was difficult for him to learn because of his strong fear of rejection and abandonment. When he was very young, I wrapped him in a blanket tightly during times of out-of-control crying. Around age two and three, I began holding him in a strong-arm hold to keep him from hurting me or himself. Then as he grew older, I let him cry and scream out his anger in his room (while sitting in his chair), first ensuring his safety. Now he can better soothe himself during frustrating moments, but he continues (with much less frequency) to revert back to his old ways of disorientation and loss of control.

A lack of nurturing and adequate holding can be detrimental to a baby's emotional security. Holding is essential for a baby who experienced a lack of touch and caresses in his or her early months. More importantly, nutrition plays a significant part in the normal developmental stages of a baby or child. A lack of the necessary minerals and vitamins will interrupt normal development. Orphanages that are not well funded might not have adequate formulas and milk supply for babies. However, much of the time, these initial delays are due to the institutionalized child not receiving enough specialized attention to encourage and develop his or her developmental skills.

All of the developmental delays noted above will affect a child's ability to eventually learn and perform in school. However, if there is not a serious medical issue involved, it is important to understand that these delays can often be overcome in time with the proper nutrition and committed, loving adoptive parents.

Medical problems

We took the counsel of our agency and had a medical expert evaluate our son's medical records and screen a videotape for any possible visual medical problems. Since we requested a child with minimal physical problems, we did not anticipate any serious issues identified with our child, but we wanted to be prepared in case one surfaced. Like most institutionalized children from Eastern Europe, our son was thought to have rickets, a Vitamin D deficiency.

Even though rickets is a mild condition and easily treated, my heart ached for our child. The thought that my child was halfway around the world and not getting the proper nutrition grieved me because there was absolutely nothing I could do about it at that time. Thankfully, my pediatrician did not see any evidence of rickets upon his initial office evaluation, conducted within one week after returning to the states.

Upon returning home, we were required by our agency to initiate a series of lab tests on our child to rule out any major problems common to internationally adopted children. Even though this was at times tedious and uncomfortable for him, we knew it was necessary, so that when minor symptoms of colds and allergies began to occur, we could rest assured that major problems such as typhoid, tuberculosis, AIDS, intestinal parasites, hepatitis, or other blood diseases were not masking themselves in the cold and flu symptoms.

Fetal alcohol syndrome is a potential problem with some overseas, abandoned children. Most of the time, symptoms of this disease can be detected in a video by the trained eye of an expert. I urge prospective adoptive parents to rely on the expertise of a trained medical doctor to identify this problem. If fetal alcohol syndrome is diagnosed, then making a decision on whether to take the referral or not can be a difficult one. In addition to seeking God's wisdom and direction through prayer, seriously look at your current family situation and determine how this disease might affect everyone in the long term. God's healing power is big and He does perform miracles, but everyone involved needs to agree to bear the burden together.

Orphaned children certainly have a disadvantaged start

in life. However, in this day and age, much information and help can be obtained in dealing with each new challenge. Issues may manifest, disappear, and then manifest again several times during the lifetime of an adopted child, but we need to remain hopeful and confident of their future.

Prepare for the worst

Preparing our hearts and minds to accept the absolute worst scenario in an adoption situation helped us to not place false expectations on our adoption. So when the trials came, we were not shocked and were more able to cope with the situation. Conversely, when the blessings came, we were more able to greatly appreciate them as well.

Timetables

Adoptions are rarely performed on our timetable. Even though we believed God was directing each step of the way in our adoption process, at each bend in the road we experienced unexpected delays and problems. In August, through photographs and video, we were introduced to our Romanian child, but we did not travel to Romania to bring him home until the following April. At the time, it was not unusual to wait four or five months for Romanian adoptions to process, but extraordinary circumstances occurred within the country's government, turning this into an eight-month delay. Our home study was completed and approved within a few months of submitting our application, but by then the summer months had arrived. The Romanian government, like many European governments, close operations in the summer for a few months' holiday, tacking on additional months before the adoption could be complete. From the time we submitted our application until the time we brought Valentin home, about fourteen months passed.

Medical profile

In the beginning stage of filing for adoption, we were asked to complete a child medical profile questionnaire. For the first time in the process, we were faced with the possibility of raising a less than perfect child. Even though biological children are not always physically perfect, I had not considered all the implications minor and major deformities might have on a child's life. We were asked questions as to the severity of different medical needs we were willing to accept in a child. Some of them were correctable and some were not. We were asked to respond to medical needs like the following with a yes, no, or willing to discuss (WTD):

+ Hemophilia
+ Other blood disorders
+ Cerebral palsy
+ Spina bifida
+ Polio
+ Wheelchair confined
+ Learning disability
+ Developmental delay

+ Mental retardation
+ Fetal alcohol syndrome
+ Malnutrition
+ Hyperactivity
+ Chronic diarrhea
+ Fecal incontinence
+ Autism
+ Physical or sexual abuse
+ Kidney malfunction
+ Urinary incontinence
+ Partial hearing
+ Totally deaf and no speech
+ Heart defect requiring surgery
+ Webbed fingers/toes
+ Clubbed feet
+ Missing fingers/toes
+ Birthmarks
+ Burns
+ Albinism
+ Cleft lip
+ No speech
+ Blind
+ Partially blind
+ Poor vision
+ Allergies
+ Diabetes
+ Epilepsy

Together, my husband and I discussed the severe disorders, and we agreed that we were not able to accept an untreatable disorder in a child. The process also forced us to consider whether we were willing to accept the known as well as the unknown disorders. I believe the unknown is more difficult to accept, because an unknown disorder can manifest itself at any time during the child's life. Most internationally adopted children have little to no medical history available about their parents, giving way to all sorts of possibilities. However, it is important to keep this in the right perspective. Even for biological children, unusual medical conditions can surface without a trace of history in the family. This was the case for my husband. At fifteen he was diagnosed with a rare form of muscular dystrophy, an untreatable and degenerative disease. No one in his family history had ever been known to have this disease. It was a biological abnormality. However, despite his disease, God greatly blessed his life of 44 years. He went on mission trips, owned Christian bookstores, earned his doctorate, married, became a popular Christian marriage and family therapist, authored a best-selling book, traveled and spoke at seminars, and for a few short years, was a father to a son. And because of my long-term and intimate relationship with him, I learned many invaluable lessons about trusting in God from one day to the next for His great grace and mercy.

While we were visiting the baby orphanage in Braila, where my son lived for four months of his young life, we met a baby his same age with a heart condition. The caretakers at the orphanage were very concerned about the baby potentially crying out of control because he could lose his breath, turn blue, and possibly experience heart failure. His adoptive parents from France were scheduled to arrive in a few days and had prepared to immediately return home for heart surgery to be performed on him. This beautiful boy was very blessed to have the opportunity to live a long and happy life because of parents who decided to love him despite the risk of heart disease.

Develop a connection by preparing a lifebook

I believe one of the adoption books we acquired during our time of waiting initiated my thoughts about a "lifebook," sometimes called an adoptive child's scrapbook. By the time we submitted our application to our agency, I felt fairly confident that our baby was either already born or was conceived and developing inside an expectant mother's womb. As we waited, I desired to grow close to our baby and missed being able to experience life together.

I believe the lifebook began to build a connection between our future child and us in several ways. First, it provided a way for me to document our child's developing life story. Second, it provided a tool to link our child's past, present, and future life. Additionally, the time I spent putting the scrapbook together kept me focused on thinking about how a baby would change our lives and how the baby would affect our existing lifestyle.

A lifebook is designed to reflect both the child's birth culture and adoptive culture. I collected pictures reflective of both our immediate and extended family. In this way he was introduced to family members he did not often see. While abroad, you may want to buy postcards, maps, and flags, and save tickets, menus, and any other paper tourist-type items that will pique interest in your child later on as you leaf through the book together.

A lifebook is one of the best ways to help a child maintain a sense of identity. It also can contain as much information as possible about a child's birth family, foster families, reasons for moving, letters from birth parents, etc. The book is designed to change and grow over time as new information is added, as the child's life evolves, and as earlier information is reviewed and expanded.

Another suggestion to help the child connect to you and your family is to begin journaling as soon as you have made a decision to adopt. This will give the child greater understanding into what was happening in your lives during the time of his or her adoption. Include your thoughts and feelings when significant benchmark dates occur such as INS approval, home study approval, matching, issues regarding delays, court dates, and most importantly, the first meeting. Sharing the lifebook becomes a way to both connect your child to his or her birth culture, reinforce his or her own unique identity, and most importantly, show your child just how much he or she is loved by you.

Lifebook contents:

Excerpts from the personal adoption journal

Agency application

Agency correspondence

Home study approval notice

For international adoptions:

> INS application for adoption
>
> INS approval notice
>
> Agency supplied child videos
>
> Agency supplied child photos
>
> International medical records
>
> International birth records, health certificates
>
> International court documents
>
> U.S. Embassy records
>
> International passport
>
> Photos of trip
>
> > Foster home and family members
> >
> > Orphanage and caretakers
> >
> > Birth city
> >
> > Hospital
> >
> > U.S. Embassy
> >
> > Hotel
> >
> > General tourist places
> >
> > Restaurants and shops
>
> Child's personal photo album
>
> Collection of items from trip:
>
> > Postcards of sites

    Postcards of hotels

    Hotel brochures

    Plane tickets

    Restaurant menus

    Flags

Child gifts: one gift for each 18 years of birthdays

Baby shower photos, gift lists, and cards

Adoption records

Birth parent information

Caregiver information

Friends left behind

Foster care information

Correspondence from well-wishing family members

Develop a life story

For decoration in my son's new room, I hung a blanket with a pattern of the world's continents with each country printed in a different color. Romania was purple, and from the very beginning of his life with us I began telling Valentin his life story. I started by pointing to Romania and telling him that he was born next to the Black Sea. I continued by telling him how God picked him out to be our special little boy. I reminded him how Mommy flew from Texas across the big Atlantic Ocean to Romania. And then I said, "I rode in a van like Daddy's from the airport to where you were living. Your foster mother was a nice woman who took care of you until I picked you up to take you to your home in Texas. And do you remember when you met Daddy in the airport in Texas for the first time?" With my finger, I trace the flight on the map from Romania through London and then to Houston. He is very familiar with this story, and now he traces the path on the map with his own finger.

Shortly after I returned from our trip, I prepared a photo album with pictures of his foster parents, social worker, translators and others who were with us. I included pictures of his birth city and its surrounding buildings and sights. Valentin loves to thumb through the album and takes great care in looking deeply into the face of each person in the photos. Having an amazing memory, he knows the names of each one. He says very little as he leafs through the book, but I know his mind is absorbing and remembering some details. I leave the album and lifebook where he can retrieve them whenever he wants. When he first arrived, he looked through them more frequently than he does today.

As the years pass, I plan to add more age appropriate details to his life story. I am careful to not overwhelm him with too many details right now. I believe keeping it simple and truthful is the best way. Early on he asked few questions, but now at age five, he wants to know more about where he came from and more about his birth parents. I believe it is important we prepare him now and not shock him with his adoption story later.

Prepare the family by managing their expectations

Too many adopted families are naïve and believe that the people within their family circle and community will be unconditionally accepting of their adopted child. In our increasingly multiethnic cities and towns, this is becoming less of an issue, but the potential for rejection within your own family remains.

After our decision to adopt was firmly planted in our hearts and minds, we began preparing our immediate family members. We tenderly approached each one, asking for their thoughts and concerns about our decision to adopt. We greatly desired their support and encouragement, knowing their influence would be important to the success of our decision. Because of her son's genetic disability, my mother in-law told us God had prepared her for the possibility of her son adopting a baby someday. She conveyed to us that she had prayed for years that God would allow him to have children, and she believed this adoption was the answer to her prayers.

As each new development occurred within the home study, the matching process, and the preparation for travel, we kept our family members informed, just as if we were taking them through the development of a nine-month pregnancy. I believe everyone felt involved in our process. My mother collected articles and news information for us about other internationally adoptive couples. I asked her to help me shop for educational toys and clothing needed for the trip to Romania. I volunteered my mother-in-law to locate books that would help a toddler integrate into our American culture and language. My father attended training seminars with us to learn about international travel and adjustments institutionalized children experience. He felt involved in the process and was a great source of support and encouragement throughout, and this prepared him for when he and my stepmother accompanied me to Romania to bring Valentin home.

Adoption may at first seem alien to some family members, so invite them to be a part of the home study and introduce them to the caseworkers. They can put relatives at ease by helping them understand how they can be supportive to their children and grandchildren. I suggest that prospective adoptive parents make available to their family members articles, books, and magazines about adoption. It is also important that you keep them up to date on what the child's life is like during the waiting process. If adoptive parents can reach out to their family members, they can help create warm and loving connections that can be meaningful in their children's lives forever.

Adoption education can teach the implication of hurtful language. Words such as "real parents," "natural child," or "children of your own" do not describe the loving quality of family relationships in an adoptive family. It is important to learn "positive adoption language." To distinguish between a child's two sets of parents, it is preferable to use "birth mother," "birth father," or "birth parent" to describe the people who conceived the child.

Adoption is not a condition or a disability. When referring to a child's adoption, it is appropriate to use the past tense to indicate the way in which a child entered the family, such as: "Jonathan was adopted," not "Jonathan is adopted." The decision made by the birth parents should be referred to as "choosing adoption," or "making an adoption plan," acknowledging their responsibility for this action. It is best to avoid terms such as "giving up" a child or "putting a child up for adoption," since these are far less positive and more emotionally charged.

Adoption education should extend beyond the family to the community, where all involved need to become more educated and sensitive to the subject. Ministers, teachers, and school administrators all are affected by an adoption. And as adoptive parents, we can help educate, counsel, and model our child's acceptance to our communities.

It is important to understand that even with the proper preparation and education, some family members in your child's life may never fully accept him or her, and these members may never be able to admit their lack of acceptance. Their belief systems about nonbiological children may be rooted in denial, false judgments, and generational sin that extend beyond anything we can identify or fix. It is my experience that these attitudes might not surface initially, but over time they can be reflected in certain peculiar behaviors and statements that portray partiality toward biological children. Protect your child as much as you can from their biased words and attitudes, but the best response you can have is for your child to witness your reaction delivered in truth with the love of Christ. And pray that these family members' hardened hearts will someday be softened. Ultimately, it is they, not your child, who will lose out in the experience of a good relationship.

Everyone working together will help facilitate a successful adoption. An adoption that is celebrated and acknowledged within the community as a wonderful gift from God makes way for a successful adoption.

CHAPTER 7

ARROWS OF DOUBT

AFTER OUR ADOPTION, MANY DIFFERENT EMO-
tions and questions began to build in my mind. However, I
believe it is accurate to say that biological parents also respond with similar concerns and doubts about their abilities to effectively parent. Elisa Morgan spoke to moms on
her MOMSense radio program one morning saying that
MOPS International (Mothers of Preschoolers) staff member Cyndi Bixler recently shared how God kept her focused
on "what matters." She said:

"Mom, to our children, we are a storehouse of
knowledge. But what do we really need to know? I don't
know lots of stuff. But I do know some. I know that I'm
a mom. I know I'm married. I know that I have a job. I
know that each day, whether as a mom, a wife, or a
minister at MOPS International, what I do matters. Other
than that, I'm still figuring it out. I don't know what my
children will grow up to be, whether I'll outlive my
husband or he will me, if I'll live in my present home in
my old age or some other spot. What do I know? I know
some stuff, but not a lot.

But I've been thinking. While it's important that I
know the truthful, real stuff of life, is it what I know

that really matters? In talking to the people around him, those who followed him both for what he was doing and those who hung out because of who they thought he was, Jesus said, "You will know the truth and the truth will set you free." To "know" means to be informed about. Ah, but to "know" is also to be "acquainted with." That's more personal. This kind of "knowing" implies a relationship. So—are we acquainted with Jesus?

Most of us readily confess, "What do I know?" Maybe the real issue is not what we know, but rather, Who?"[1]

Prospective adoptive parents naturally will have many questions, doubts, and concerns about raising a child who is not their biological child. I've addressed some of these common questions and concerns.

Can I love a child that is not my own?

I believe this question is the most frequently asked question and concern of potential adoptive parents. However, something about the helplessness and innocence of children draws a heart of compassion out of us. And by caring for and meeting the needs of a child, we are naturally drawn closer to that child.

What if I don't "feel love" for the child?

Love is manifested in many different ways. Love is not

just a feeling but requires active participation on our part. If you wait for love to be felt, you might become disappointed when it does not surface quickly. However, as we nurture, pray, and care for a helpless infant or child, our daily duties will eventually bring us to have deep feelings for the child. Several newly adoptive parents I've talked with have told me that their feelings of love for their child grew over time even though these feelings were not instantaneously experienced.

Can I put someone first that I don't know?

God begins to work within the hearts of new parents in a mysterious and wonderful way that cannot be described completely with words. However, I can testify to how God worked in my life for me to be able to sacrificially give of myself to my new son. I don't have personal time like before, but I don't resent giving it up. There is so much that I want for my son emotionally, spiritually, and physically that I will gladly do what is necessary to make sure his needs are met, because I am the only one who really knows his needs.

Should I adopt a toddler when I wanted a baby?

Our plan to adopt a toddler was not deliberate, but it turned out to be in our best interest. Some parents may feel as though they will miss out on the infancy of their child with a toddler adoption. I had some of these concerns in the early stages of the adoption process, but after Valentin arrived, I began to feel blessed to have him at whatever phase of life he was in. I began to accept that his needs were far more important than my need to cuddle and care for an infant. And I know he is better off in his current circumstances. Whatever has happened to him is in the past, and I can do nothing to change it, but I can greatly influence his future by helping him to heal from his past, and I am committed to do this for as long as it takes.

Will I attach quickly?

The ability to attach quickly to a child depends on both the parents and the child. And attachment will be delayed for both parties if the child has developmental or physical issues. Toddlers who have enjoyed healthy and stable caregiver relationships seem to have fewer attachment difficulties, but they continue to need support in recovering from their grief over the loss of these relationships.

Some adoptive parents have told me their child attached to them many months before they attached to their child. However, like myself, others have told me they attached with the child immediately upon meeting the child. I believe this is similar to the encounters biological parents have as well. And sometimes when the child's temperament is similar to the parent's, attaching occurs more quickly.

Some adopted babies, toddlers, and children will not make eye contact with their new parents because they are not prepared to cope with the intimacy eye contact generates. An older child may have shame issues that need to be dealt with. Give your child time to develop good eye contact. With babies, feeding them in your arms and looking at them during this close time will help them to develop intimacy. With older children, having a good daily regiment of floor time activities where the parent and child are on equal eye level will help develop greater eye contact.

I believe it is unpredictable to say when you will attach, but eventually the attachment will occur. Most parents agree that it happens within the first three to nine months. I knew my attachment with Valentin was real when his whimpers during the night woke me from a dead sleep into a state of consciousness within a millisecond. I have always been a heavy sleeper. I have slept through many thunderstorms when trees were toppled and power lines downed without my knowing anything had occurred during the night. It was not until my sweet but strong-willed son entered into my life that my sleeping habits changed forever. Only God could cause the tiny whimper of a child to pierce the solitude of peaceful sleep.

What if my child initially rejects me?

Initial rejection by an adopted child is common. He or she may not respond to physical affection or may pull away from physical affection. The new environment and new people frighten newly adopted children, but for the sake of survival, they also feel compelled to try to "fit in." The younger the child, the easier to transfer trust and affection, whereas older children with a history of physical, emotional, or sexual abuse are less likely to embrace their new environment with excitement and ease. Their past dictates a style that is more reserved and cautious about entering into new and unproven relationships.

Thankfully, our toddler embraced me from the beginning. He somehow knew that I was there to take on the role of "Momma" in his life, and he was very happy to receive me in that role. Several weeks after returning from Romania, my son and I were at the checkout counter in the grocery store when he thrust his little finger in my direction, and with a huge grin on his face blurted to the cashier: "That's my Momma!"

Will I be able to accept rejection from my child?

Once the honeymoon period is over, the child often will feel comfortable enough to begin acting out in ways that cause some parents to feel rejected. These children are testing their parents' commitment. Rejection can come in many different forms, and children who have been rejected have learned how to hurtfully reject others. They may be disagreeable about the things you do to try to make them comfortable. Depending on the child's past, kicking, hair pulling, hitting, biting, scratching, and screaming are typical behaviors. They have not developed appropriate coping mechanisms with which to vent their anger and hurt, so they do what comes naturally. Usually venting comes in the form of physical abuse or verbal abuse by lashing out against the people who care most about them. When this occurs, it becomes our responsibility as parents to teach them more appropriate coping mechanisms. But even healthy, biological toddlers show some of these characteristics while working through frustration and anger.

Most of the time my son is very loving, affectionate, and playful, but he has acted out in some of these ways over the years. His inappropriate behavior most often occurs when he is tired, hungry, and frustrated about not being able to effectively communicate his feelings. However, underneath these issues is a tender heart with a huge amount of compassion, which is common among children with difficult pasts.

Helping a child work through these issues must be done with the love of Christ and with much patience and perseverance. It is important that we demonstrate consistent attitudes and in-control behavior to our child. Stand firm against their strong opposition, never giving in to their fits of temper while always letting them know you are in complete control of the situation. An exhausted parent may feel tempted to give in to her own frustrations, but for the sake of the child's best interest, we must seek God's strength to rise above this temptation.

Am I prepared to go the distance?

Looking back on our first year with our newly adopted son, I realize now we were both in a state of emotional and physical shock. We lost much sleep while Valentin struggled with night terrors and memories of his past. He woke sometimes four and five times each night with shrill, high-pitched screams. After each sleepless night, he would cry and whine most of the next day for something he couldn't express or verbalize. He demanded to be held almost all day long, desperately trying to find security. He experienced severe separation anxiety if I was not by his side constantly. During the first year, we were challenged more emotionally, physically, and spiritually than we had ever encountered in our lives. But gradually things got better. Many months into the ordeal, Valentin's night terrors subsided and his whining diminished. We learned to be thankful for the small changes and rejoiced with Valentin as he progressed. We loved our new son very much and would have done anything in the world for him, but after the first year, our energy was expended and we were totally exhausted. Not all adoptive parents of toddlers experience the intensity of the separation anxiety and night terrors that we did. Our situation was a bit unusual. However, newly adoptive parents need to be prepared to battle it out for the long haul.

Will my spouse love the child as much as I will?

I felt love for Valentin before I met him, so when our eyes met, I believe there was instantaneous attachment. For my husband, it took about three months for mutual feelings of attachment to develop, and when Valentin began allowing the two of them to make eye contact for long periods of times, I knew he felt safe with my husband. They began interacting on a deeper emotional level, and my husband felt he was included in Valentin's inner circle. To facilitate attachment, my husband sang songs to Valentin during his first few weeks at home and taught him to sing the basic "C" music scale of la la la la la la la la. Valentin delighted in being sung to by his Daddy and tried to imitate him from the start. He also loved to ride on his daddy's wheelchair and hold on tightly as they drove fast through the house. These special times spent together over the first few months greatly helped facilitate trust and a deeper bond.

What if I or my spouse is disabled?

My husband was confined to an electric wheelchair. He was not a paraplegic, but he had very limited strength in his arms and legs. With the extra assistance of a caregiver, we managed over the years to develop a routine for morning and night tasks. But we were somewhat concerned about how our new child would relate to the wheelchair and to his disabled daddy.

With the international dossier that was mailed overseas, we sent photos through the agency of ourselves and our home. Each photo was carefully labeled so the Romanian foster parents could put names with faces of family members, friends, and pets. I copied the photos using a color copier and put each page of photos in a protective plastic sleeve. We hoped they would be used to prepare our child before my arrival in Romania. To help minimize the shock of his wheelchair, we provided various photo scenarios with my husband working, relaxing, traveling, and speaking in seminars. This seemed to help, because our son was never afraid of the wheelchair or his daddy. We were quite amazed at how well he acclimated to both. Valentin never hesitated to climb up onto his daddy's chair and into his lap, and he was much encouraged by us to do so. It did not take long before he was nestling in his daddy's lap for comfort and security. He developed extraordinary coordination and balance as he adapted to the sudden movements and motion of the motorized chair.

At Valentin's age of 16 months, it was not appropriate to explain the details of my husband's disease. I've listed five practical steps in preparing a child for a parent's disability:

1. Prepare the child before the initial meeting.
2. Do not deny or overlook the disability.
3. Do not overemphasize the disability.
4. Reinforce safety precautions.
5. Reinforce security and deemphasize fears.

In the early days, I was uncertain as to how his father's disability would affect our new son, but after about six months of living with the handicaps of his father, his behavior was very telling. I watched him act with an unusual level of servanthood. He also demonstrated a great level of sensitivity to the needs of those around him. Most children his age are too self-absorbed to notice the needs of others, but because of his background and his father's disability, God was using these challenges to mold godly character.

General feelings of inadequacy

Before plunging into an adoption, all of your questions and concerns should be closely evaluated. Fear and hesitation can be fairly natural when we are staring into the chasm of the unknown. However, when your thoughts turn into irrational fears wrapped in doubt, it is time to remember God's promises:

Stand firm in God's truth:

Become familiar with the source of truth and trust in His ability.

"Trust in the LORD forever, For in GOD the LORD, we have an everlasting Rock" (Isa. 26:4).

Don't fear:

Fear is not from God, and He wants to deliver us from it.

"For you have not received a spirit of slavery leading to fear again, but you have received a spirit of adoption as sons by which we cry out, "Abba! Father!" (Rom. 8:15).

We cannot fully serve God when we are serving fear.

"To grant us that we, being delivered from the hand of our enemies, might serve Him without fear" (Luke 1:74).

"There is no fear in love; but perfect love casts out fear, because fear involves punishment, and the one who fears is not perfected in love" (1 John 4:18).

Reject the lies:

Remember what good things God has done for you.

"For the Mighty One has done great things for me; and holy is His name. And his mercy is upon generation after generation toward those who fear him" (Luke 1:49-50).

When we do not give way to the lies, we can experience God's peace in the middle of a storm.

"The steadfast of mind Thou wilt keep in perfect peace, because he trusts in Thee" (Isa. 26:3).

Remain focused on one step at a time

Any one of the many obstacles we encountered during our adoption process could have put a stop to our plan. However, we continued to believe God was with us, working on behalf of us and little Valentin.

December 26, 2000

There have been stumbling blocks along the way with Don's birth certificate being lost. Then the state department would allow only ten pages at a time to be sent to them for conselorization.

Because of all this, we did not make our deadline to

be able to set a court date on Dec. 15. Another wait, and now with the holidays, it is indefinite. Nicole wrote us an e-mail with encouraging words saying, "Tell them Valentin will wait as long as needed, he will go to them . . . I'm sorry about the delay with the conselorization."

What a blessed statement of encouragement. God is with us, and His hand is still on Valentin. I'm so sorry we will miss his first birthday. It was hard enough not having him here for Christmas. But we know God's timing is perfect! We will be able to spend many birthdays in the future with him!

January 25, 2001

The "super authenticated" document that Romania wanted was mailed from Dallas this morning. It took almost three months to accomplish their request of conselorization. Also, with the problems centered on our presidential election, things slowed down at the state department at the end of the year. Then with the Romanian elections, their government process slowed also. We had a "double whammy" of delays.

January 31, 2001

The document was delivered to HUG International in Bucharest this morning. Now it is all out of our hands. We will wait to hear from Nicole regarding a court date.

February 14, 2001

I spoke with Buckner today. They said the RCA (Romanian Council for Adoption) would meet at the end of the month. Hopefully our adoption will be reviewed to assign a court date at that time.

February 28, 2001

Per Buckner, the RCA did not meet this month and will be meeting mid-March.

March 12, 2001

Buckner called and the RCA met this morning. Our adoption was approved and the paperwork involved was forwarded to Braila. A court date will be set on Friday to finalize the adoption. It is getting closer!

March 15, 2001

Finally! A court date was set for March 26 (in 11 days he will be ours!). We are making travel plans for the last week in April. We are currently waiting for the birth certificate and passport to be issued, which will take a few weeks. Buckner asked for the name we wanted on the birth certificate.

March 26, 2001

We are officially parents! The Romanian Council on Adoption met in Bucharest today and finalized our adoption. What a miracle! It is truly happening. We will soon go to get our little boy.

March 28, 2001

We received our travel dates to Romania. We will leave April 21 and return to the United States April 28. We will spend two days in Braila, then the remainder of the time in Bucharest. One last night will be spent in London.

I urge you to not go this road alone. Adoption should be a celebrated event and not conducted in secrecy. You will need the support of those around you who know you best. Our much-needed encouragement always came at just the right time and gave hope to my heart as I waited to meet my son.

+ CHAPTER 8 +

THE FISHBOWL DELIVERY

"NO ONE COULD HAVE PREPARED ME FOR THIS," says Kathy Erickson of Freedom, Wyoming. "Nothing I had read or seen could describe the exquisite joy of my soul. I'm a mother! Me! Oh heart, be still. Who is this sweet, pink face—so fresh from heaven—peeking out from beneath her blanket cocoon? Oh, God, you have such faith and trust in me. Please stay close and whisper in my ear the things I need to know. I want to do my best."[1]

My husband and I faithfully prayed every day for our son from the moment we chose adoption until I left for Romania to bring him home. This time period was about one and a half years. The power of the Holy Spirit working through our united prayers created a bond between our child and us, even though he was living halfway around the world.

No privacy

Upon completing the extensive agency questionnaire, we began to feel an invasion of privacy. Personal questions were asked to help the social workers understand us better as individuals and then as a couple. Our general life history was laid out before perfect strangers. However, we believed that our agency operated in an extremely confidential and professional manner with our personal and private information.

Their reasons for uncovering the details of our lives were multipurposed. First, the information clarified our motives and desires for a child not only for the agency, but for us as a couple. Second, the agency is required to operate within strict state guidelines, and the maintenance of their reputation and license is critical to their future success. They must verify that we fit the profile of being honest and responsible citizens. Third, the agency must ensure the adoptive home and parents will provide a safe, loving, and nurturing environment for the child. We cooperated with our social workers to ensure the process was conducted to their satisfaction.

Onlookers

Being disabled, my husband did not fly to Romania with me to pick up our child and bring him home. Even though I desperately wanted my husband to be a part of the process, we both knew there would be very few provisions for his wheelchair in Romania as it is not a handicap-accessible country. He remained home, and we kept in contact almost daily as to the development of our adoption finalization process. I invited my stepmother, father, and a close friend to make the trip with me, believing that I needed as much support as I could find from family and friends. When difficulties with the finalization process began to occur in Braila and again in Bucharest, I was very grateful I had the support of people close to me. Our agency had provided us with the additional support of two translators and one driver for the duration of our stay. We also had the support of four HUG Foundation representatives. These women and men were blessings to us as we traveled and attempted communication with the different Romanian officials. Everyone had a servant's heart, ready to meet our every need without hesitancy.

However, there were times I felt like I just wanted to be alone, at least for one hour, to get to know my new son. Everyone was full of advice and constructive criticism about my parenting methods. I was told Valentin needed more clothes on, or he should not eat sweets before his meal, or that he should not be allowed to explore the hotel as much as he wanted to, and I should be learning more Romanian so I could communicate with him better. My head was swimming with everyone's advice. They all meant well, but I was overwhelmed with the constant opinions of ten people.

Looking back on the situation, I am thankful to have had so many people providing support. However, being a quiet and private individual, all of the different sources of influence were daunting.

Our first meeting

When I met our son for the first time, I felt as though we were already a part of each other's lives. Here are my journal notes from my first visit with Valentin in Romania:

April 23, 2001

I met Valentin today! What an awesome experience for me! He is so beautiful and incredibly smart. His foster parents are grieving severely about letting him go.

He likes music and watching TV. He loves to hold the remote control and dance to the music. He understands everything spoken to him in Romanian. When he is not quite sure of a phrase or word spoken by his foster mother, he squinches up his forehead. He will have a determined look on his face that says, "I want to get this right!" When he is asked "Where is Momma?" or "Where is Nana?" or "Where is Romy?" or "Where is Dana?" he will point at that person. It was incredibly special that he knew I was his Momma from the very beginning.

He knows the meaning of "not allowed" in Romanian, which is "nui voya." He will shake his finger at whatever is not allowed. Tonight we went to the restaurant in Braila, and he sat on a stool with the man in the band with the microphone. Valentin loved the attention everyone was giving him. He is a real entertainer. He danced and moved to the music and laughed at the audience. What a gift he is!

The shock of instant toddler

What was new to me when I met our son was not the child. The work involved in caring for our child was new. And carrying a 27-pound baby in my arms was shocking to my body! Most parents have the experience of gradually developing arm muscles to carry a baby as he steadily grows from six or seven pounds to 30 pounds. My arms ached for weeks. And I was not used to devoting my full and complete attention to the ever-wandering hands and feet of a toddler.

I have thought many times about how parents of twins or triplets manage their babies' energy with their own physical limitations. And I have discussed with many new parents about how unprepared they felt to care for their new, helpless baby who requires an insurmountable amount of attention with continuous demands. My conclusion is that rarely do new parents feel prepared to meet the needs of a new baby. They require almost 24 hours a day, seven days a week, of personalized attention. It is even more difficult when this new baby has a past and is a stranger with whom you cannot yet relate.

Expect problems and delays

We expected the embassy to accept our power of attorney, allowing me to sign for my husband in his absence. However, this document was not acceptable to the embassy. In addition, a faxed copy of his signature was not legal representation. This detail caused a major delay that I was not prepared to handle.

We also experienced a delay in obtaining Valentin's certificate of adoption, further delaying the remaining processes. These circumstances brought me to my knees before the Lord. I claimed these promises to help comfort me:

"The Lord will keep you from all harm—he will watch over your life; the LORD will watch over your coming and going both now and forevermore" (Ps. 121:7-8).

"The LORD watches over you—The LORD is your shade at your right hand; the sun will not harm you by day, nor the moon by night" (Ps. 121:5).

April 25, 2001

We are still in Braila. There has been an indefinite delay in our schedule. The Romanian council on adoption has not issued the certificate of adoption. Recently the government changed the process without HUG's knowledge. It now takes longer than ten days. Without the certificate, we cannot have the passport. Without the passport, we cannot see the embassy medical doctor. We may receive the certificate on Friday if we have favor with the council. Then on Monday we can go to the embassy for two appointments in one day. We will then be able to leave Tuesday for the states as planned. We decided to wait out our stay in Braila since the cost of hotel and food is much less expensive here. Don is trying to rearrange our tickets in case we need to leave a few days later.

April 26, 2001

Rika took me today to the director's office of the Baley's orphanage in Braila. She was sympathetic to our problem. She made a few phone calls to politicians in the area, but no one seemed to be able to accomplish anything. Vali (Nicole's mother) is still working with the RCA to get the certificate by Friday. If we get it by then, we may be able to leave for Bucharest as planned; otherwise it will not be until Tuesday and all our plans will need to be rearranged.

Please, Dear Lord, Maker of heaven and earth, send your heavenly messengers to walk this process through the RCA and embassy so we can take our baby home. Have mercy on us and expedite the process. Remove the blockage of any evil that may be working against us. Jesus, I acknowledge that you are in control, not the RCA, and not the enemy. I recognize your Holy strength and power and I ask you to demonstrate these qualities in this situation. Thank you for your great love and care for us. Amen.

The uneven exchange: the caregiver's story

We were blessed for our child to live in a foster home with a Romanian Christian family. Foster parenting was fairly new in Romania as there are few qualifying families with enough space, time, money, and emotional energy to take in an orphan. God placed our Valentin in a home with an older couple with college-aged children. The mother was in her 50s, experiencing the "empty nest" syndrome. Her husband was older, retired, and supportive of her endeavor. Valentin was her first foster child. She was in the video sent to us that was made shortly after he arrived in her home at seven and a half months old. It was obvious to me from the video that she was good to him and she loved him. Valentin was in the care of the foster family for about nine months before I arrived on the scene. His foster mother had been prepared by the social worker for my pending arrival, but when I got to the apartment to take Valentin, she was understandably grieving her loss.

While I was going through those few minutes of information exchange, I selfishly wanted to take my child as soon as I could and depart from the scene. I believe her grief was driving her to overly scrutinize my attempts to mother my new son. I could tell she thought I did not provide warm enough clothes for him. These moments were tense and uncomfortable as she and I had differences of opinion as to how my son should be dressed. She proceeded to put his thick red tights back on underneath his heavy overall jeans, but the agency had prepared me for this possible conflict, so I remained compliant and cooperative to do what she thought was best for Valentin.

I prepared a list of questions for the foster mother to help assist me in understanding my son. Due to all of my excitement and distraction, I did not get through every question on my list. However, the more questions that can be asked and answered, the better able the new adoptive parents will be to problem-solve and troubleshoot as issues manifest later down the line. My questions consisted of the following:

1. What name does he have for his caregiver?
2. What are his favorite foods?

3. Has he been sickly?

4. When does he nap and go down for the night?

5. How long does he nap?

6. How long does he sleep at night?

7. What is his daily routine?

8. What is his potty routine?

9. What is his bedtime routine?

10. What are his favorite toys?

11. What Romanian words does he say?

12. What names does he call his foster mother and father?

13. What kind of milk does he drink?

14. What is his bath routine?

15. What upsets him or what does he fear?

16. What soothes and calms him?

17. What comforting words does he like?

18. Does he sleep by himself?

Intently, he listened and watched his foster mother talk to me. He was quite perceptive of her emotions and was picking up on nonverbal cues from her as to how he should respond to his new mother. She told him I was his new Momma as she stroked my arm. Picking up on her sadness and grief, he began to whimper and cry. She wept and had much difficulty saying good-bye. He knew that I was taking him from her, but it was all right because she had said so. However, he was still somewhat unsure and scared. He reached for her as we left the apartment, but quickly and quietly settled into my arms as we stepped into the elevator and watched the doors close on the only home he had ever known.

It was several months after I returned to Houston and settled into motherhood that I realized how unappreciative I had been toward his foster mother. In Romania, I showed graciousness to her and told her how grateful I was for her, but it wasn't until much later that I realized the vast significance her role had played in our lives. It was because of her that Valentin was able to adjust to our family so quickly. He had experienced family life for nine months in her home, so being introduced to our home was much less shocking than coming directly from the orphanage. It was because of her love for him that he would know the love of a mother and is able to relate to me so easily. It was because of her tender care that he received good nourishment and healthy eating. It was because of her diligence that he was taught how to use a fork, spoon, and cup and could sit and eat with adults. In love, she had spent much time teaching and disciplining him.

I thank God for her love and attention to my son. To the best of her knowledge and abilities she had prepared him for his new life. What a great blessing she was to Valentin and our family! She gave so much of herself to a little boy who would soon leave her home for another country and whom she would probably never see again. This was not an even exchange on her part. She gave of herself sacrificially and without expectation of anything in return. This is the kind of sacrificial love our heavenly Father has for us. I had a lot to learn from her about sacrificially giving to a toddler. It did not come as easy to me as it seemed to have come for her.

The initial adjustments

The first night with Valentin in the hotel room in Braila was an unusual experience for both of us. He slept beside me in our twin bed. In the middle of the night he woke up in the dark room with big, frightened brown eyes looking directly into mine and screamed. I could see sheer terror in his eyes. He immediately crawled over me, slid off the bed and ran to the door. As I picked him up a few feet before he reached the front door of the hotel room, he had his right arm elevated with his index finger pointing toward the door, whimpering helplessly. The only way I could console him was by holding him close and singing to him. This was just the first of our many sleepless nights together.

Valentin wanted to eat and drink all day every day from the moment we received him. I had brought to Romania canned milk supplemented with calories, vitamins, and minerals recommended by our pediatrician as well as cans of Vienna sausage, Cheerios, breakfast bars, apple juice, and other canned baby foods. Valentin did not appear malnourished, but when he ate he would cram his mouth full of food as fast as he could, until it would not hold one more tiny crumb. His cheeks would puff out like a chipmunk's.

We had been told by our agency to watch for signs of "food hoarding." At the time we did not think of this as food hoarding, but later we realized this was how a 15-month-old, institutionalized baby hoards his food. We attribute this act to when he was in the orphanage and not getting enough food to become satisfied. And while we ate pizza with his foster mother, I witnessed her limiting his food intake. She did not want him to eat until he was full, fearing he would get a tummy ache. I've never experienced not having enough food to eat for a meal, but many Romanians experience a shortage of food daily.

At first, Valentin hated to have his diaper changed. He was fussy, wiggly, and cried furiously at each changing. Bath time also was a new experience for him. Our American method of running water generously into a large tub and setting the child totally naked there by himself was frightening to Valentin. I don't believe he had ever had what we call a "bath." The first few times I tried to hoist him over the side of the bathtub and into the water, he screamed loudly. By the third bath attempt, he felt more comfortable and began to like playing in the water with his toys.

Before I left Houston, I had purchased a pair of white high-top shoes in the size I guessed he was wearing and brought them to Romania. He loved his white shoes and the security and confidence they gave him when walking. The only shoes he had previously worn were sandals and soft booties, so he stood tall in his sturdy new shoes!

April 25, 2001

Valentin is learning new things every day we are with him. He has learned to wave bye-bye. He has learned to hold the railing on the stairs in the hotel as he walks down them. He slept through one night and woke only once for a few short minutes. He is not responding to his name, neither Valentin or Jonathan. It is by his choice, I think. He seems bewildered at times, but always happy. He comes to me for comfort and knows I am his Momma. I sense he is still unsure about acknowledging my new position in his life.

We went shopping in Galatz today. He rode in his stroller very well. Yesterday he began riding in his car seat. He does not like the confinement. I have seen no one in Braila with car seats or strollers. Babies are carried around close to the mother's body until the child can walk securely on his own. He falls asleep quickly in the seat once the car is moving. I was told his foster mother took him in the car and for rides on the train occasionally.

Yesterday we went to the baby orphanage in Braila. The caretakers remembered him. They called him "Pipi" and were pleased to see him. The women caretakers kissed him and pinched his cheek. He was very happy and seemed to remember them even though it had been nearly nine months since he had lived in the orphanage. The head nurse gave him a play phone he found in the waiting room. On the way out of the courtyard, she picked him some Lily of the Valley flowers growing wild and handed the bunch to him. He gripped those flowers for most of the morning until the buds wilted and fell off their stems.

The language barrier

An international adoption almost always requires overcoming a language barrier. Even at a few months of age, babies know to respond to certain words and phrases. A foreign language at first will generate frustration and insecurity, but they will quickly overcome the barrier. I wanted to have some form of a functional vocabulary to connect with my son, so I bought conversational tapes to hear the Romanian language and learn a few words with which to communicate.

At fifteen and a half months, our son had begun to speak a few Romanian words and understood most Romanian that was spoken to him. After listening to his foster mother talk to him, I had learned a few comforting words to which he had responded well in Romanian. But when I said them with a different accent, inflection, and tone of voice, he acted as though he had not heard the words before. For the most part I was clueless on how he liked to be comforted. The soothing phrases, words, and sounds American mothers make to their babies were foreign and unknown to my son. However, I began repeating the same phrases, words, and sounds over and over, day after day, until they eventually became familiar and comforting to him. The few weeks we spent in Romania with the translators greatly helped in his transition to English. This provided additional security to both of us as we headed home without translators.

In the very first days of our introductions, I held Valentin tightly and gave him lots of kisses and hugs. Physical affection and closeness breaks down many language barriers, especially for children who are starved for a parent's touch. And I was enjoying being able to provide every little ounce of affection I could give!

+ CHAPTER 9 +

RETURNING HOME

AFTER RETURNING HOME AND SETTLING INTO A regular routine, Valentin's confidence with the English vocabulary increased. His initial attitudes were cautious, but curious, with little rebellion, and he would never let me out of his sight. However, on trips to the grocery or department store, he engaged with strangers who would listen about his new kitty cat, Elmo doll, bedroom, or anything else of importance that came to mind.

The honeymoon of adoption

It was reassuring to hear people say, "He looks just like you!" It seemed impossible to me that an Eastern European-born baby could look like me, but in many ways he did. He had the same color and texture of hair I had as a baby, and just like me, his sensitive nature is reflected in his eyes and facial expressions. I believe that is what people are really seeing.

All new parents experience a time of learning about their new baby. We want to know our child's likes and dislikes, comfort needs, and personality types so we can bond with them. With adoptive parents, some catch-up time is needed to bond with the new arrival. With a newborn, it is inherently easier to control every step of his or her new beginning, sheltering the child from possible pain and difficult predicaments. But for an adoptive parent of a child with a history, establishing appropriate boundaries for yourself and the child is more complex. Some adoptive parents want to overprotect and treat their new child as if he or she has a disability. But I encourage you to not enable your child's limitations or overcompensate for them. This can potentially delay your child's ability to grow effectively into a new environment. By encouraging your child to engage in new activities, you will empower the child with the self-confidence and courage needed for future life skills.

I found it very difficult to discover a healthy balance between overprotecting my son and giving him too much freedom and control. The newness of a child was exciting and rewarding after longing for one for so many years, and in the early stages of settling into our family, Valentin was very compliant and good-natured. We told people he was the "perfect child." At the same time, we were allowing him to exhibit permissive and unrestrained behavior because I did not understand the concept of controlled freedom. I realize now that I established a shaky foundation of loose boundaries, forcing me later to redraw firmer boundaries of what was permissible and what was not.

In his book *Adopting the Hurt Child*, Dr. Keck states that first-time parents might have unique adjustments to make due to their initial fantasies of what parenthood is all about.[1] New schedules, household rules, and laborsome tasks may at first be overwhelming to new parents. He says they may need to reconcile their unrealistic attitudes and assumptions about their roles as parents before they experience their own sense of security in their situation.[2] Ironically, as my confidence in my ability to parent increased, so did my son's ability to effectively learn self-control and appropriate boundaries.

Establish initial security with the familiar

In orphanages, the fortunate children have consistent caregivers, but for most, the care they receive changes with each work shift and day. Therefore, institutionalized children look for other consistencies imbedded in their surroundings, and not in people, to provide them with a sense of security. Smells, pictures on walls, architecture in the room, and other inconsequential items become important to them.

When this security (even though it is a false sense of security) is taken away, extreme fear and anxiety can set into the psyche of the child. This fear and anxiety are exposed in disconcerting behavior as the child enters a fearful situation and can't focus on something familiar. This is an example of why our agency suggested we take articles of clothing and bedding with us from our child's previous environment to provide some sense of familiarity and security to our son in his new home.

Develop security with new associations

Orphans do not acquire possessions, and upon our arrival in Romania, we noticed Valentin did not use a pacifier, have a favorite blanket, or carry a favorite stuffed animal or toy. He seemed to not have an attachment to any material thing. We gave him new blankets and toys that he enjoyed, but he was indifferent to identifying them as "newfound security." He liked to carry things in his hands, but he did not need to carry the same "things" every time. He eventually did become attached to his "sippy cup" with juice. Before my arrival, he had been eating with adult utensils and drinking from adult glassware. He began to sleep with his new cup and cry for it in the middle of the night when it was lost in the covers of the bed. Later, during times of high anxiety and frustration, Valentin would ask for his "appa," the Romanian word for water and the new label for his cup. This new association became the newfound security he needed when he became anxious or scared.

Identify food favorites and intolerances

Food adjustments were difficult. Valentin did not have a natural ability to regulate his desire for food by his hunger pains. He would not eat for long periods of time, refusing food until he was ravishingly hungry. Unfortunately, by this time, his blood sugar was so low that he would demonstrate severe mood swings coupled with bad behavior. Once I understood this direct correlation, I insisted he eat at least two bites of food from each item on his plate at each scheduled mealtime whether he wanted to or not.

When he did eat, he liked to make eating a long, drawn-out event. He was not accustomed to eating in our fast-paced manner or digesting the processed foods Americans consume so much of these days. He developed allergies to French fries and fried chicken nuggets, which caused little raised red bumps to appear on his face and arms. He preferred hard salami and sausage to our hamburger meat, roasted chicken, and pork. He loved eggs and cheese of all kinds, and on good days wolfed down two scrambled eggs for breakfast. His familiar hard rolls and stale toast were more interesting to him than fresh bread and biscuits. Rice and potatoes were his staples, not pasta. Drinking pasteurized cow's milk presented problems with gas and diarrhea, and we finally settled on soy milk to alleviate these problems. He did not like our applesauce; I believe he was used to having his foster mother make her own pureed applesauce from scratch.

One day I discovered that he loved soup. The best part of the soup for him was to crumble as many crackers as possible into his cup and pick them out with his fingers. He also loved hot cereals like oatmeal and Cream of Wheat because cold cereal is not widely available in Romania. He did, however, learn to love eating Cheerios from a plastic bag and drinking his soy milk separately. And when he decided he liked peanut butter sandwiches, I believed he truly had become an American child!

Preparing appealing and interesting food was an experimental process for us for quite some time. I finally settled into three or four staples that I gradually expanded into other food areas over the months and years.

Incorporate a highly structured daily routine

The popular phrase, "A place for everything and everything in its place" is an important concept to put into action. The adopted child especially needs consistency in knowing where his belongings are kept. Toys, books, clothes, and personal items should all have a "home" so the child can predict their whereabouts. The consistency and predictability this kind of structure provides their environment will help build trusting relationships. And the trust that develops will establish a healthier foundation for learning.

The honeymoon is over

As the weeks began to turn into months, Valentin began more fully manifesting his pain and suffering from the past. His little body underwent physical and emotional changes along with the adjustments to a new family, culture, country, and role in life. Within four months he had grown eight new teeth. Within nine months he had grown five inches and put on six pounds. Parents of biological children deal with the normal physical growing pains associated with teething and developing muscle tone, but parents of institutionalized children usually have periods of time needed to play "catch-up" in the child's physical and emotional growth.

The wounded heart

Nancy Newton Verrier explains her observation of adopted children's struggles in this way:

> When this natural evolution is interrupted by a postnatal separation from the biological mother, the resultant experience of abandonment and loss is indelibly imprinted upon the unconscious minds of these children, causing that which I call the "primal wound."[3]

In my observance, this template of rejection created by separation from the birth mother can cause many challenges in raising an adopted child. It is important that adoptive parents gain understanding and knowledge about the potential difficulties. Most importantly, the adoptive parents need to work through their own rejection and abandonment issues before they can successfully guide a child through his or her grief and healing.

Harboring secrets from the adopted child can be destructive. Secrets may acquire the power to cause pain, shame, and self-doubt in a child. God's Word cautions against secrets; "For nothing is hidden that shall not become evident, nor anything secret that shall not be known and come to light" (Luke 8:17). Nothing can be hidden from God. Secrets should be brought from darkness into the light of truth in the right time, and with a heart of compassion.

Attaching

The most critical aspect of an effective adoption is the attachment process between parents and the adopted child. In the book *Raising Adopted Children*, Lois Ruskai Melina gives the following advice about attachment:

"The infant who formed an attachment to his biological or foster parents before he was placed may look for that person in times of stress. This doesn't mean that he is rejecting his adoptive parents. In time, he will come to recognize them as his primary caretakers. Searching can be a good sign; the child who has been able to form attachments in the past will form new attachments more easily than the child who has never felt an attachment, because he has already learned to trust."[4]

And Mary Hopkins-Best describes the possible characteristics of attachment problems specific to toddlers:

+ Developmental delays unexplained by known disabilities
+ Unusual patterns for eating and sleeping
+ Resistance to being comforted and cuddled
+ Ambivalent behavior toward parents
+ Selective rejection to one parent while accepting the other
+ Scarcity of distinction between parents and strangers
+ Raging and aggressive behavior
+ Extremely negative and controlling behavior

+ Unorganized behavior and poor impulse control
+ Missing or extreme separation anxiety
+ Premature independence
+ Unnaturally positive behavior[5]

The best way to facilitate attachment with your newly adopted child is through simple tasks such as feeding, smiling, eye contact, touching, cuddling, stroking, and kissing. However, some children are at first less likely to accept physical affection. For these types, meeting their physical needs by providing plenty of food and a comfortable and safe environment can produce trust and help to facilitate attachment. The length of time it takes for attachment to occur varies because of the age of the child, past abuse issues, number of previous attachments, personality, and comfort level with his new parents. It is not possible to predict how long attachment will take with a newly adopted child; however, according to Dr. Gregory Keck, if attachment has not occurred after one year of being in a stable home environment, something is wrong.[6]

Because our son had nine months to attach to his foster mother, who was a loving and affectionate caregiver, he had developed an initial trust that he was able to quickly transfer to us. However, he did grieve the loss of his foster mother and "looked for her return" for several months.

Children with attachment issues are especially vulnerable to feelings of abandonment during the beginning stages of adjustment. They are still insecure and will often test our trustworthiness. For about two months after Valentin arrived, my husband and I were cautious about allowing our son to spend time alone with other people until he demonstrated that he assuredly knew we were his parents.

Lois Ruskai Melina says it eventually is important to allow your children to attach with those outside of the immediate family.[7] I had been praying for someone special to come into the house on a regular basis to provide breaks for me during the week. I wanted someone I trusted that could give me time to catch up on missed sleep and allow me to perform basic duties around the house while Valentin was being cared for. The answer to this prayer came through a young Romanian teenage girl who recently had been adopted by one of our church members. She and my son took to each other immediately, sharing their language and culture. She performed her job beautifully and gave me much-needed breaks to keep the refrigerator stocked, laundry done, mail sorted, and other household tasks accomplished. God had truly answered my prayers.

Grief

Unexplained sadness, depression, and anxiety in a child often points to underlying grief. The grief is most likely due to an early abandonment experience. The loss of identity, culture, friends, caregivers, or a sense of unfamiliarity may trigger a reaction. All children are unique in how they manage and cope with their losses. Some need more help than others in dealing with past issues, and most unsocial behavior will need to be addressed by a professional. It is important to recognize grief in your child and allow your child to grieve. We need to assist with teaching our child to learn and develop new coping skills. Nancy Newton Verrier, author of the book *The Primal Wound*, offers this advice in regard to a grieving child:

> "When one has suffered a loss at the beginning of life, before conscious memory, there is a need to work through this loss in order for the person to function well later in life, both personally and professionally."[8]

My son's grief came in the form of whiney and clingy behavior. Initially, he expressed few emotions and his facial expressions were flat. He demanded that I give him physical affection. Sometimes he pointed to the door or the next room and made grunts and groans as if he were looking for someone. Even after he learned the English language well enough to tell me what he wanted, he only cried, groaned, and pointed. He was inconsolable and unable to verbalize the pain he was feeling. When this occurred, I held him in a blanket like a baby, gave him juice to drink, sang to him, and stroked his hair or rubbed his back until he was calm. His grieving periods eventually became fewer and further between.

In his early grief, I believe my son was looking for someone he hoped would return. This was demonstrated one day when we were on the playground with other parents and children playing around us. He clambered down the slide after another little boy who was being coached by his father. Valentin closely watched this man's face by leaning way over the edge of the slide as if he were looking for something deep behind his eyes. This man was tall with a dark complexion, and as he began to speak in his native Spanish language, my son connected eye to eye with him. Unexpectedly, Valentin let out a cry and pointed to him saying, "That's my Daddy." This incident reaffirmed that he is always on the lookout for someone from his past.

Stages of adjustment

After an adopted child arrives in a new home and new country, a parent will need to be prepared to recognize stages in the child's adjustment to the new environment. Each child's progress will vary according to age, sex, and background history. According to Jean and Heino Erichsen, the following six emotional stages will be identifiable in the newly (internationally) adopted child:[9]

1. **Compliant:** Children's initial presence in an adoptive setting is one of submission. The child has little to complain about, as the child is good.

2. **Curious:** Children leap into our culture and imitate the fads of children around them. Children might tell their new mother or father by words or actions, "You're not my parent; you can't tell me what to do."

3. **Disoriented:** Children's new culture is in conflict with their old culture concerning what is expected of them. They may reject the new family or become aggressive. The child is frightened and defensive.

4. **Experimental:** Children try to cope. They acquire the more appropriate behaviors of peers, become involved with the family, friends, and schoolwork.

5. **The All-American Boy or Girl:** At this stage, children reject their old culture more vehemently than in stage three. They don't want to talk about their past. They say they are a regular American kid.

6. **Adjustment:** Children achieve a balance by knowing who they were and who they are in order to function in the United States, in their new family structure, and with their new language.

I believe these stages also can be applied (with slight modification) to domestic adoptions of non-infants. And for toddlers, the above stages are less clearly defined. Their actions more than their words will define each phase. For our son, the compliant stage was very clear and defined, but as his time with us progressed, the curious and disoriented stages were muddled together. This was partly due to his age and partly due to his stubborn nature. As Valentin moved from the experimental stage into the adjustment stage, he tested our trustworthiness by pulling out all the stops. He held nothing back, allowing us to witness his joy, pain, and insecurities—sometimes all at the same time.

No particular formula or method exists by which to predict or manage each individual child's issues and manifestations of those issues. Most of the time, adopted children enter into a new household with an unknown past that predicted an uncertain and hopeless future. The child's past cannot be erased, for it has become etched into his unconscious and sometimes conscious memory. Our challenge as adoptive parents is to help our children learn to manage and cope with the pain of their past so that they can put it behind them and have a stable, secure, and hope-filled future. Just like our Heavenly Father desires for us, we desire our adopted children to share in His abundant life and inherit all we have to offer emotionally, spiritually, and physically.

+ CHAPTER 10 +

INTEGRATION

This Hole In My Heart

My Mommy says I have a hole in my heart.
It feels like a deep, wide and bottomless pit.
Sometimes I don't know it is there
When I'm playing and jumping and talking to you.
But, then it will come, like a thief in the night,
Like a trigger on a gun.
I will be pulled to great depths where it is black with no sun.
My eyes will glaze and my thinking is hazed.
Where is my other mommy?
She has vanished into the depths.
I go searching in vain.
In my fear and pain,
I scream out for help, but no one can hear!
They think I am not obeying when I need reassurance.
Please help me God!
Will You fill this great hole?
With Your love and understanding?
And will You help Mommy and Daddy to know what to do,
When I'm lost inside myself
Looking for You?
—Kimberley Raunikar Taylor

This poem reflects the hurting heart of my adopted toddler who does not yet cognitively understand the nature of his grief, sadness, and anxiety. Toddlers, in general, have many unexplained anxieties in reaction to their world, but an adopted toddler struggles even more. He has a history that is unknown and unexplainable to his limited understanding and capabilities.

I wrote this poem one morning after a long night filled with my son's night terrors and anxiety. I was left tired and grievous over the condition of my young son's troubled heart. The poem speaks from his position of being unable to verbalize his thoughts and feelings. He is crying for unconditional love and acceptance first from his birth mother, only to eventually realize that it is only God who can fill the hole in his heart. As he goes through this intense struggle for acceptance, he is asking for patience and understanding from me, until he can sort through his grief and anxiety.

Compliancy and curiosity stages

By the time I returned home to Houston with Valentin, we had spent two weeks in Romania together. The entire time we were there he was given around-the-clock attention, kept busy with talking, playing, and people teaching him new words and sharing new experiences. Our translators were speaking Romanian and English to him regularly. It was a good transition for him to have both languages spoken for a few weeks. He is such a smart and quick child that he began learning English before we left Romania. He could say words like Momma, Daddy, kitty-cat, cracker, juice, and cookie.

He remained happy and content to be with all of us as we traveled in Romania. He laughed, smiled, and was very willing to please us, but he also was cautious and reserved. He showed some insecurities and lacked confidence with his new environment. He knew I was his primary caregiver and began coming to me for comfort, but was indiscriminate about letting anyone hold him, feed him, and entertain him. For about three to four weeks after arriving home, he continued to be fearless about strangers and new people. However, it was almost overnight that he became less friendly with strangers and insisted on being taken care of only by Momma.

Language development

Once we were at home and on our own, and because of necessity, we quickly overcame the challenges of the language barrier. Valentin was eager to relate and communicate, and tried hard to please us with his new words. By reading to him, talking to him constantly, and watching children's videos, he understood English fully within a few months of his arrival. His speech was never delayed because of the second language, but many foreign-born children do experience some delay.

A friend of mine who adopted two babies from Vietnam verbally explained every task she performed with her babies, talking it out as she was in process of each task. Even though her son and daughter were only three and four months old, she spoke to them as if they knew exactly what she was saying:

"Let's change your diaper because it is wet and uncomfortable to you. Let me place you on the changing table. I'll take off your pants and shoes so I can then take off your diaper. This wipe will be a little cold, but it will help clean you off. Let me put this diaper rash cream on your bottom so your rash will feel better. Here is your new diaper. This is the front side and this is the back side of the diaper. Let me lift you up while I position the diaper under your bottom. The tabs will stick to your diaper on both sides so it will not come off. Here are your pants and shoes, let me put them back on again."

Her children quickly adjusted to the English language and today both are very verbal.

Disoriented stage

After three to four months of compliancy and curiosity, my son moved into the disoriented stage with full force. We had difficulty determining whether this stage was because of his background or the fact that he was entering the "terrible two" phase. He became more clingy and whiney during the day, and his nightly sleep patterns grew more unstable.

Where am I?

Night terrors are more than just bad dreams. They are a child's experience of pure terror during vulnerable sleeping hours. Valentin's night terrors were quite disconcerting, to say the least. At first we were not sure what was happening. I thought he was having bad dreams, or that he was having a gaseous response to the food he was eating. As the problem escalated, I finally realized that what I had read about night terrors was actually occurring with our son.

Valentin would fall asleep next to me without a problem, but he would wake up within four to five hours crying and whimpering. Sometimes he would violently kick me as if trying to liberate himself from something, like a blanket or troublesome sock. I would try to talk to him and console him, but he would not respond to my comfort as he would during the daytime, acting as though he did not know who I was. His face would be tightly contorted with his eyes slightly open with a painful look. He screamed and cried like a baby does, instead of the more mature cry of a toddler. Sometimes he would slide off the bed and run out of the bedroom and down the hallway screaming and crying. One helpful friend suggested that when this happened, I should wrap him tightly in a blanket and rock him. I began doing this, and he began to respond positively.

Other people told us he needed to stop sleeping in our bed. We tried putting him in his own crib, but after a month or so of being in his own bed, his episodes became more frequent. Instead of once or twice a night, they would occur three, four, and sometimes five times during one night, lasting anywhere from fifteen minutes to one and a half hours. No one in the house was getting any sleep during these difficult times. Each time I would get up and try to reassure him that I was his momma and that I would take care of him.

After months of desperation, one such episode prompted me to get out his magnetic drawing board. I drew pictures of myself, his daddy, and him as well as our home, church, and friends. By transferring his focus to the drawings and my words, he was able to move out of his disassociation. I ended the drawing sessions by singing "Jesus Loves Me," and most of the time, he was then able to talk to me in his normal, sweet voice and go back to sleep. Also, I found that reading Ps. 91:4-14 and praying this scripture over him quieted him:

"He will cover you with His pinions, and under His wings you may seek refuge; His faithfulness is a shield and bulwark. You will not be afraid of the terror by night, or of the arrow that flies by day; of the pestilence that stalks in darkness, or of the destruction that lays waste at noon. A thousand may fall at your side, and ten thousand at your right hand; but it shall not approach you. You will only look on with your eyes, and see the recompense of the wicked. For you have made the LORD, my refuge, Even the Most High, your dwelling place. No evil will befall you, nor will any plague come near your tent. For He will give His angels charge concerning you, to guard you in all your ways. They will bear you up in their hands, lest you strike your foot against a stone. You will tread upon the lion and cobra, The young lion and the serpent you will trample down. Because he has loved Me, therefore I will deliver him; I will set him securely on high, because he has known My name."

Unexplained anxiety and fears

Valentin was very sensitive to loud and unfamiliar noises. When the vacuum cleaner ran in the next room, he would shake and tremble in fear. When I turned on my hair dryer, he cast a startled look in my direction. And every time I turned on the washing machine, the dryer, the garbage disposal, or any other household appliance, I warned him first to prepare him for the noise. Even now, after several years of talking to him about the vacuum cleaner and the hair dryer, he continues to be startled by these sudden loud noises.

These kinds of unusual responses to sensory input can also be triggered by textures, touch, sudden movement, taste, smell, and temperature. Children with attachment issues can be highly sensitive to their sensory environment and respond in inappropriate and highly exaggerated ways. Dr. Keck says, "The early trauma experienced by children who have attachment difficulties impacts every aspect of their existence. One area commonly affected is the sensory system—the part of the brain that organizes and processes sensory input and uses the input to respond appropriately to a particular situation."[1] Some children respond well to very hard hugs, almost body crushing hugs. They like to feel the extreme sensory input received from these kinds of hugs, not understanding that others do not always want to receive this form of affection. On the other hand, some children with sensory integration issues will be highly sensitive to any kind of touch, cowering and moving away even from a loving hand laid softly on their shoulder. Some children experience difficulty feeling the elastic waistbands in their underwear and tags inside shirt collars. These minor irritations to most children become highly exaggerated frustrations to children with sensory issues.

Sometimes the simple requests I made to Valentin caused him to quickly escalate into extreme fits of frustration. His personality normally is gregarious and outgoing, but when he became agitated and fearful about performing the simple task of picking up paper off the floor, I knew something was working in his thought process that wasn't normal. I would be firm with him about following through with my request, but I also gave him grace in these situations. When he became calm, I talked the situation over with him and asked questions about his feelings. He didn't always know why he was frustrated, but I tried to create a safe and secure environment for him to learn and talk about his feelings.

There were times he absolutely refused to be restrained

by his car seat. He kicked, scratched, and screamed to keep from having to be locked into the seat. Other times he wanted the seat belt to be as tight as it would go and fussed when it was too loose. His behavior has sometimes been irrational, leaving me exasperated without answers as to how to correctly handle the situation.

Separation anxiety

For about six to nine months after he came home, Valentin wanted to be held from the minute he got up in the morning until the minute he went to bed at night. At mealtimes he insisted on sitting in my lap to be fed. Then for naps and nighttime, he wanted to fall asleep only in my arms. I believe he was afraid I was going to leave him and not be there when he woke up. Upon waking, he immediately would scream and cry loudly, demanding I come to rescue him from the loneliness of his bedroom. When I tried to leave a room to go to the bathroom or to get something from the next room, he would run after me screaming and crying. He could not be left alone for one minute without his fear manifesting. Loneliness is a very fearful feeling for Valentin, and he went to extreme measures to not be alone.

Separation anxiety touches the deep wounds of abandonment and loss. Going to mother's day out, the church nursery, or being left with a babysitter can be very disturbing to a newly adopted child. Each time the adoptive parent departs, something in the child's unconscious memory reverts back to the first abandonment experience with his birth mother. He will experience this memory on the same physical and emotional level that it was initially experienced.

There are ways to reduce the separation anxiety level of a child, but most importantly, as his parent, you must consistently reassure your child that you will return. And then you must return when you say you will. Use a reference your child understand. I always said something to the effect of: "I'll be back after nap," or "Momma will return after your snack time," or "After your lunch I'll come back to get you." Toddlers can understand these time references much better than specific times.

Aggressive behavior

Expressing anger through aggression is a common way adopted children express sorrow and loss. In an agitated state of mind, the child has a low frustration threshold and will demonstrate an exaggerated response to his environment. When behavior seems out of proportion to the situation, it is most likely a reaction to an old feeling triggered by a recent event. It was difficult at first, without knowing Valentin very well, to know if these were normal toddler tantrums or a response to past trauma. And sometimes this aggressive behavior was triggered by overstimulation in his environment. Most all of the public children's arcades are no place for a child prone to aggression. The loud and sudden noises, chaos, and confusion in these establishments have always triggered negative and agitated responses from my son, and we avoid participating in activities at these places.

By becoming aware of your child's early warning signals, his aggression can be better managed. Just a very few minutes before the anger fuse blows, I usually witness some warning signs such as obsessive whining, irrational demands, and clingy behavior. To help him, I validate his feelings by saying things like, "Settle your body down, and talk to me about how you feel. Are you sad? Are you angry?" Sometimes I open our discussion to talk about Valentin's feelings by saying, "Does your heart hurt today? Tell me about what hurts you. Tell me about your angry feelings. Sit on my lap and let's talk a minute." These statements and responses usually defuse his initial signs of aggression, but if his behavior continues to escalate, I firmly let him know that this is not appropriate behavior, and there will be consequences if he continues to act out his aggression.

Abnormal eating

In our home, in restaurants, and in malls, I regularly discovered my son sitting on the floor scavenging for food. He wasn't just picking up something he had dropped; he was actually looking for anything tasty other people had dropped. At two years old, when he grew hungry at home, his first choice was to be sneaky and head for the pantry or refrigerator before asking me for food. He seemed to believe that finding food was his responsibility.

Dr. Keck says that one sign a child has suffered early

neglect, abuse, and deprivation is his approach to food: "Depending on his history, the child may steal, hoard, gorge, purge, or even refuse to eat. Food related problems are connected to the child's uncertainty of being fed when very young and are a sad reminder of the effects of neglect and abuse."[2]

It has been a long transition for him to believe he is not responsible for getting his own food. Even today, at the age of five, we continue to work with his need for indiscriminate food scavenging.

Healing through holding

It is unlikely that my son received the holding and comfort he needed as an infant. Orphanages rarely have the time and personnel to meet all of their babies' physical and emotional needs. These special times of helping Valentin through his grief and aggression were healing for me as well. I was able to experience some of his infancy stage with him that we both missed, further deepening the attachment between us.

+ CHAPTER 11 +

ALL THE WAY HOME:
EXPERIMENTAL AND
ALL-AMERICAN STAGES

VALENTIN WAS SLOW TO INTEGRATE WITH OTHER children. I could tell he sensed differences between them and himself. Some of his first experiences with American children were on the playground. He rapidly reverted to the behavior of a very young toddler when other children came around. He would not talk to them, only giggle and act sheepishly timid, even though he was quite capable of conversing with them. The differences he noticed made him feel insecure. The children smelled different, were more assertive and aggressive, looked different, and talked more than what he was used to experiencing in the orphanage. He watched them closely to understand their behavior and motives.

When I gave another child any form of attention, Valentin exhibited high levels of jealousy towards them. During these moments, I reinforced to Valentin that I loved him, and that I care about other children as well. It took several years before his jealousy subsided.

Struggle for control

One of the ways a child will attempt to prevent future loss is to try to be in absolute control of every situation that occurs in his or her life. The battle for control can be exhibited in such behaviors as rage, rejection, and rebellion. At the root of the struggle, the child is desperately seeking unconditional acceptance and love but doesn't know how to communicate this message effectively. We need to be prepared to handle unreciprocated love by depersonalizing his or her rejection of us. By understanding the origin of the behavior, we can better remain steadfast in our commitment to love our child. We are making an impact on this child's life, but the fruits of our labor may be long in coming.

We concluded that Valentin was a strong-willed child shortly after he arrived. He had a plan and a purpose for almost everything he wanted to do. His feet were so quick that he would act on his plans before I knew what was happening. And when I tried to interrupt his plans, he became furious and obstinate.

When he wasn't being whiney and clingy, he would exhibit a surprising amount of independence. He did not like strollers, so when we went to the mall, he insisted on walking and did not want to hold my hand. He would run ahead of me, sometimes 200 feet, before he would stop and look back. All of my calls to him were to no avail. The same little boy who had fearfully clung to me earlier that morning in the comfort of our own home was acting fearless and risky in a strange place.

My son's great need for control often showed in his bowel movements. Without warning, he would run away from me, or scream and cry, demanding that he be let loose from his car seat, stroller, or highchair. This was his strange way of saying, I need to go "poop" in my diaper. He would scream and yell if someone tried to come near him to change his diaper sooner than he was ready. Until I finally caught on to this behavior, we almost always ended up in a heated struggle for control of the situation.

One day Valentin's teacher told me he had not obeyed in preschool, and I later asked him why he did not obey his teacher. His blatantly honest answer was, "I do not want to." I said to him, "Jesus wants you to obey your parents." He retorted: "No! I don't want to!" I repeated to him, "I'm in charge, and when I'm not there, your teachers are in charge. You must obey your parents and your teachers." The next Sunday on the way to church, I overheard him talking to himself in the backseat. He said, "I'm not in charge. Momma is in charge."

As parents, we are the ones in charge, and we must stay calm during a tantrum or control struggle, even when our children are badly acting out. This can become wearisome, but the earlier in life we let them know who the boss is, the fewer problems with control related issues we will have to deal with in later years.

The effect of new losses

When Valentin was almost three years old, I began gathering up our old clothes, food, and toys that he no longer used and took him with me to the drop-off site. He was very disturbed when the workers came out to our car and began taking my personal items and placing them on loading carts. He said to the men, "That is my Momma's! Do not touch my Momma's things!" And when they took his own bag of clothes out of the car, he began to whimper and cry.

Unknowingly, I had triggered memories from his past. Lois Melina says, "Subsequent losses, even minor ones, can trigger memories of past losses, especially if the person has not fully grieved for the previous loss. . . . Anyone who experiences a significant loss is likely to feel new losses more acutely. The death of a pet, a broken toy, or a friend who moves away can provoke grief in a child that may seem out of proportion to the actual loss."[1] As parents, we will make mistakes, but none that are irreversible when we acknowledge them and seek our Lord's forgiveness.

Though Valentin's past made giving a confusing experience for him, it also made him more willing to give than most children his age. Later that day, we stopped at the local mission to give away food. When we arrived at the facility, a line of mothers and children were waiting to get their daily quota of food for their families. I told my son that the food we were giving them would help these children to not feel hungry. Valentin wanted to play and talk with the children in line with their mothers, and he was very eager to give away food so they would have enough to eat.

A few months later we began preparing Christmas boxes for children in orphanages living in other countries. He went with me to pick out toys to place in the boxes. He wanted them to have stickers, crayons, balloons, and battery-operated fans. He also picked out warm socks and gum. When we visited Santa a few weeks later, I was concerned at how he would react to this strange man with a white beard in a red suit, but he was not afraid. After Valentin settled onto his lap, Santa asked him what he wanted for Christmas. It was quite surprising that the first words out of my son's almost three-year-old mouth were: "There are boys and girls who do not have toys and clothes. They need toys and clothes. I gave them mine." I'm sure that Santa had never heard that one before! I don't believe he knew how to react. He just nodded and looked over at me. I winked at him and said, "He is a very sensitive child and looks out for the best interest of others." Despite my lack of understanding and empathy concerning giving away his toys and clothes a few months earlier, God allowed it to be used as a good experience for my son.

Bubbling to the surface

One day, about 18 months after we brought him home, Valentin verbalized for the first time the troubled part within himself. (This may have been the little baby that would cry out at night during the night terrors.) The three of us were watching a new videotape featuring a large group of four-to five-month-old babies lying on the floor on white fluffy cloud pillows. Some were crying, some were smiling, and some were fearful about their environment. Valentin whimpered and cried, crawled into my lap, and pointed to the video. With somberness and sadness in his voice, he said to me, "Those babies don't have mommies and daddies." The image on the video must have triggered a memory of when he was lonely and afraid in the orphanage. And now that he could use language more effectively, he was able to unveil the hurt and pain in his heart. These precious times of new revelation can be used as a healing tool for the troubled places of a child's heart. I explained that these children did have mommies and daddies, and that they were in the next room where we could not see them. This seemed to give him the peace he needed to rest his troublesome thoughts, at least for a while.

When he was three, we invited a play therapist to our home to assist Valentin and me with the concept of "floor play." We were hoping to learn how to share control and uncover some thoughts and ideas floating around in his head, giving us a clue to some of his need to control his environment so strongly. To my great surprise, the first day she came, he pulled out the Play-Doh and picked the yellow, red, and blue colors as his favorites. (Incidentally, these are also the colors of the Romanian flag.) He took the entire can of yellow and flattened it like a pancake on the table. He then took the blue and separated it into seven pieces that he rolled into individual elongated tubes. He took six of the blue pieces and placed them evenly next to each other in a row on the yellow pancake. He said, "These are my brothers." He then took the remaining blue piece and laid it next to the row of six and said, "This is me, and these are my brothers." Lastly, he opened the red can and again, he flattened the entire can of Play-Doh on the table like a pancake. He picked up the red pancake and placed it on top of the yellow with the blue cylinders. He pinched the edges of the yellow and red pancakes together to close them. Then he picked up the entire "pancake set," laid it on his chest like a baby, patted it, and said, "These are my brothers, and I have to take care of them." Most likely, he was "remembering" his time in the orphanage when several babies were placed in a crib together, either to keep warm or because there was a lack of baby beds. His extreme sense of responsibility at such a young age helped us to understand some of his need to excessively control his environment.

Training and discipline

Dr. Keck gives some very good advice to parents who have more rigid backgrounds regarding child discipline: "The fewer and simpler the rules in a family, the more likely it is that a child will comply with those expectations. Traditions, rituals, and family expectations will most likely click in as the child develops a need to become part of the group. All unnecessary rules should be abandoned."[2]

The following list contains some of the issues adopted children might be internalizing and processing that keeps them from always responding appropriately to their new environment and expectations of others:

+ Misunderstanding the seriousness of offense or behavior

+ Is dissociating and temporarily deaf to your instructions (e.g. night terrors, or mentally and cognitively reverts back to younger behavior)

+ Unexplained fears and anxiety

+ Significant confusion about cultural differences (e.g. European children are not as overly protected as American children; American restraining mechanisms such as car seats, strollers, and high chairs are puzzling)

When an unruly emotional outburst or incident occurs, wait until your child has calmed down before you attempt to reason or talk to him or her. While the child is in an agitated state of mind, he or she is not able to think or reason clearly. Make sure your child is safe. Hold a small child during the tantrum if it is necessary to keep the child from hurting himself or herself, you, or others. Keep calm yourself, and address the issue by first validating the child's feelings, letting him or her know the behavior is not appropriate, and offering an alternative (e.g. you are angry, but you can't hit me, you can hit the pillow).

Regardless of the reasons for behavior, your child should know there are consequences to inappropriate behavior, and these consequences should be administered when a child has been clearly warned of them prior to making a poor choice.

Attachment issues, separation anxiety, language and cultural barriers, and many more issues can become overwhelming to a new adoptive parent. Parents who are struggling to wrap their minds around these issues need to take each day as it comes. It is important to celebrate each accomplishment no matter how small and insignificant it may seem to you. Remember the words of Phil. 4:6-7 to encourage you when you are overwhelmed: "Be anxious for nothing, but in everything by prayer and supplication with thanksgiving let your requests be made known to God. And the peace of God, which surpasses all comprehension, shall guard your hearts and your minds in Christ Jesus."

Share your faith in Jesus

Our son came to us from a spiritually dark country with many generations of godlessness and evil rule. We recognized before Valentin arrived that he would need to establish a firm foundation and relationship with Jesus Christ. As a baby, he had not heard the Bible songs and special words about Jesus that Christian mothers whisper into their babies' innocent hearts and minds. We took the opportunity while getting to know him (and him learning about us), to also teach him about Jesus. We sang Bible songs to him, and taught him that Jesus was everywhere. We told him that Jesus made the grass and the trees and the birds. We told him that when he was scared, he could talk to Jesus so he would not be scared. He woke up one morning in our bed to the sound of birds chirping outside our window. To our amazement Valentin said, "The birds are talking to Jesus!" We confirmed that yes, they are!

Demonstrate public acceptance

I felt a need to publicly confirm our commitment to our new child, and I believed the best place to do this was in our home church. After we began to settle into parenthood, we registered for the next available spot in the baby dedication services. We desired to confess to raising our new child in a loving Christian home with Christian values and principles. Even though our church was not accustomed to dedicating toddlers, they accommodated us. Days after the ceremony, Valentin began to display an unusual new sense of security and confidence. I believe that because of our public witness and confession, he experienced a spiritual transformation within.

Identity through ownership

A change of ownership requires time to realize and know whom we are and to whom we belong. (This experience is synonymous with our salvation experience and getting to know God and His character.) From the very first day upon his arrival home, we had told Valentin that the new room was his bedroom, with his bed, and his toys. But it took a while before he felt and experienced true ownership of them. One morning, about nine months after his arrival, Valentin woke up and immediately proclaimed to me with a new excitement in his voice, "This is Vale's room! This is Vale's bed! These are Vale's toys! That's Vale's blanket!" Again, I felt like a major spiritual transformation had occurred, further deepening his sense of security and attachment to us.

The resilient child

Most children are more resilient to difficulty than we give them credit, but through all of Valentin's disruptions and transitions, he has maintained an unusually optimistic, empathetic, cheerful, and accepting attitude. Mary Hopkins-Best says, "There are some children who arrive home almost unscathed by abandonment, neglect, lack of preparation, and even by multiple disruptions in their young lives. The resilient child can survive and even thrive in circumstances that would often destroy most people."[3] The resilient child's characteristics, according to Mary Hopkins-Best, are:

+ Precociously independent; this may be difficult to differentiate from a toddler's natural drive for autonomy.
+ Mentally withdrawing or retreating; resilient children get through their difficulties usually by having the ability to temporarily dissociate from their circumstances.
+ Initiative; involves the ability to assert oneself to as-

sume whatever control one can over a situation. These children can master their environment using leadership skills, and delight in problem solving. They are able to master development tasks despite the lack of encouragement and resources normally provided by loving adults.

+ Insight, sensing, and intuition; their insight is manifested in their close watchfulness on their environment and their unusually good memory for people and events.

+ Build intimate and fulfilling relationships with others; these children can search out love by connecting with or attracting the attention of available adults at a very young age. This is done through their eye contact, touch, rudimentary language, and other engaging behavior.

+ Humor and creativity; they direct their energy into play with a happy disposition, spontaneous laughter, creative play.

+ Morality; these children have an incredible depth of understanding regarding the rights and wrongs of daily life. They show unusual compassion for their peers, and they distress when other children are hurt or frightened. They will attempt to assist other hurting children.

My son, the resilient child, seems to be innately protected from succumbing to many of the disadvantages adopted children have experienced; however, he has not been left unscarred. There are wounds that run deep into his little soul, hidden for now, only to surface later as God draws them out for His purpose.

+ EPILOGUE +
TRAGEDY SHAPES OUR FUTURE

MY HUSBAND'S, AND VALENTIN'S ADOPTIVE father's, death in January 2004 was a crushing event. At first it seemed as though all my hopes, dreams, and desires for not only my son's life, but also my own were buried with my husband. But I have no doubt that God wanted me to adopt Valentin as my son. I also believe that God worked through the brokenness to draw my son and me closer to Him. By pressing closer to God, I found the strength and courage necessary to continue on this revised path.

The night I told my son his father had died, he asked, "Who will be my daddy now?" These words, spoken in his precious voice, still ring in my ears. As my heart was breaking, I told him Jesus would be his daddy now, but he could begin praying for a new daddy. Immediately he took my words to heart and began praying every night for a new daddy, until one day, he showed up! My new husband is a gift from God, and a treasure to my child. Now Valentin has a testimony in his life's story of how God answered his prayers for a new daddy. God continues to be faithful, even when our natural eyes are cloudy and filled with tears, and hopelessness consumes our hearts. However, by changing our focus and looking with spiritual eyes, we can see that God continues to work to bring beauty from ashes.

If adoption is in your future, be obedient to God's call and let Him lead you through the process. The road will be filled with ups and downs, twists and turns, but He will shower you with blessings along the way. Remember to look for them.

NOTES

Chapter 1

1. Evan B. Donaldson Institute, *Benchmark Adoption Survey: Report on Findings* (New York: Evan B. Donaldson Institute, 1997).

2. 2000 Census Bureau. (2000) *2000 Census Report*.

3. National Adoption Information Clearinghouse (NAIC), *Disruption and Dissolution,What Is Disruption?* Naic.calib.com.

4. R.P. Barth and M. Berry (1988). *Adoption and Disruption: Rates, Risks, and Responses* (Hawthorne, NY: Adline de Gruyter).

5. V. Groza and K. Rosenberg (1998). *Clinical and Practice Issues in Adoption: Bridging the Gap Between Adoptees Placed as Infants and as Older Children* (Westport, CT: Praeger).

6. Ibid.

7. Ibid.

8. Barth and Berry (1988), *Adoption and Disruption: Rates, Risks, and Responses.*

9. Ibid.

10. Ibid.

11. Ibid.

12. Ibid.

13. V. Groza (1986), Special needs adoption. *Child and Youth Services Review*, 8(4), 363-73.

14. K. S. Stolley (1993), Statistics on adoption in the United States, *The Future of Children: Adoption*, 3(1), 26-42.

Chapter 2

1. R. P. Barth, D. Brooks, and S. Iyer (1995), *Adoptions in California: Current Demographic Profiles and Projections Through the End of the Century*, Executive Summary (Berkeley, CA: Child Welfare Research Center).

2. Ibid.

3. M. Berry (April 1996), "Preparation, Support and Satisfaction of Adoptive Families in Agency and Independent Adoptions," at p. 166, Table 2, *Child and Adolescent Social Work Journal*, Vol. 13, No. 2.

4. Ann Spangler, Belmont, Michigan, quoted in *A Love Like No Other: Joyful Reflections from the Hearts of Mothers* by Elisa Morgan (Sisters, OR: Multnomah, 2001), 56.

5. Quote made by Theresa Meyers, Port Orchard, Washington, *A Love like No Other: Joyful Reflections from the Hearts of Mothers* by Elisa Morgan (Sisters, OR: Multnomah, 2001).

6. The Poem, *Mother's Day* by Margaret Munk of Silver Spring, Maryland from *Perspectives on a Grafted Tree: Thoughts for Those Touched by Adoption*, compiled by Patricia Irwin Johnston (Indianapolis: Perspectives Press, 1983).

Chapter 3

1. Quoted from Paul Pennington and Doug Martin, Family Life Today radio ministry staff members, program for "Hope for Orphans," *If You Were Mine*, Part 3.

2. *Loved by Choice*, by Susan Horner & Kelly Fordyce Martindale (Grand Rapids: Fleming H. Revell, 2002).

3. National Council for Adoption. Adoption Factbook Publication #1077 (Washington, DC, 1989), *Adoptable Children: What Is Meant by "Children with Special Needs?"*

4. 2000 Census Bureau. (2000) *2000 Census Report*.

5. Ibid.

6. Ibid.

7. National Council for Adoption (1986).

8. Quote by Thomas Atwood, president of the National Council for Adoption (2003), *USA Today*, "Census Counts Adoptees: 1.6M Kids," by Karen S. Peterson (08/22/2003).

9. 2000 Census Bureau. (2000) *2000 Census Report*.

10. Ibid.

11. 2000 Census Bureau. (2000) *2000 Census Report*. Taken from Family News In Focus—A Web site of Focus on the Family (www.family.org/cforum/fnif/news/a0027473.cfm) (August 25, 2003), Terry Phillips, *First-Ever Report on Adoptions Available*.

12. Ibid.

13. Ibid.

14. Internal Revenue Service Publication 968. Tax Benefits for Adoptions.

15. Ibid.

Chapter 4

1. Elisa Morgan, *A Love like No Other: Joyful Reflections from the Hearts of Mothers*, (Sisters, OR: Multnomah, 2001).

2. Elisabeth Elliot, *Keep a Quiet Heart* (Ann Arbor, MI: Vine Books, 1990).

3. Ibid.

Chapter 5

1. Patricia Irwin Johnston, *Perspectives on a Grafted Tree: thoughts for those touched by adoption* compiled by Patricia Irwin Johnston (Indianapolis: Perspectives Press, 1983).

2. Lois Ruskai Melina, *Raising Adopted Children* (New York: Harper Collins, 1998).

3. Jane Bradshaw, *Name That Baby* (Nashville: Broadman & Holman, 1998).

4. Ibid.

5. Quoted from the *Oklahoma City, Oklahoman & Times* by Ann Landers (February 25, 1978).

Chapter 6

1. Mary Hopkins-Best, *Toddler Adoption: The Weaver's Craft* (Indianapolis: Perspectives Press, 1997).

2. Ibid.

3. Gregory C. Keck, Ph.D. and Regina M. Kupecky, LSW, *Adopting the Hurt Child: Hope for Families with Special-Needs Kids* (Colorado Springs, CO: Pinon Press, 1995), 48-49.

4. Ibid.

5. Ibid.

6. Ibid., 17.

7. Mary Hopkins-Best, *Toddler Adoption: The Weaver's Craft*, 111.

8. Ibid., 39.

Chapter 7

1. Quote by Cyndi Bixler from *MOMSense Radio*, a production by Elisa Morgan (November 12, 2002).

Chapter 8

1. Kathy Erickson of Freedom, Wyoming, *A Love like No Other: Joyful Reflections from the Hearts of Mothers* by Elisa Morgan (Sisters, OR: Multnomah, 2001).

Chapter 9

1. Keck and Kupecky, *Adopting the Hurt Child: Hope for Families with Special-Needs Kids*, 119.

2. Ibid.

3. Nancy Newton Verrier, *The Primal Wound: Understanding the Adopted Child* (Baltimore, MD: Gateway Press, 1993).

4. Lois Ruskai Melina, *Raising Adopted Children* (New York: Harper Collins, 1998).

5. Mary Hopkins-Best, *Toddler Adoption: The Weaver's Craft* (Indianapolis: Perspectives Press, 1997), 186.

6. Taken from a personal note by Gregory C. Keck, Ph.D. (November, 2003).

7. Lois Ruskai Melina, *Raising Adopted Children*, 186.

8. Nancy Newton Verrier, *The Primal Wound: Understanding the Adopted Child* (Baltimore, MD: Gateway Press, 1993).

9. Jean Nelson-Erichsen and Heino R. Erichsen, *How to Adopt Internationally: A Guide for Agency-Directed and Independent Adoptions* (Fort Worth, TX: Mesa House Publishing, 1997), 144.

Chapter 10

1. Keck and Kupecky, *Adopting the Hurt Child: Hope for Families with Special-Needs Kids*, 181.

2. Ibid., 39.

Chapter 11

1. Lois Ruskai Melina, *Raising Adopted Children*, 153.

2. Keck and Kupecky, *Adopting the Hurt Child: Hope for Families with Special-Needs Kids*, 135.

3. Mary Hopkins-Best, *Toddler Adoption: The Weaver's Craft*.